BEYOND

—THE—

INCORPORATION

A Startup Guide to Navigating Taxation,

Registrations, and Compliances in India

- ✓ *A Handbook for Entrepreneurs & Professionals*
- ✓ *10+ Tax savy strategies*

By

CA MEGHA JAIN

★ ★ ★

DISCLAIMER

The author and publisher of this book have used their best efforts to prepare this material. The author and publisher make no representation or warranties with respect to the accuracy, applicability, or completeness of the contents. They disclaim any warranties (expressed or implied) or merchantability for any particular purpose. The author and publisher shall in no event be held liable for any loss or other damages, including but not limited to special, incidental, consequential, or other damages. The information presented in this publication is compiled from sources believed to be accurate. However, both the publisher and author assume no responsibility for errors or omissions. The information in this publication is not intended to replace or substitute professional advice. The strategies outlined in this book may not be suitable for every individual and are not meant to provide individualized advice or recommendations.

The advice and strategies found within may not be suitable for every situation. This work is sold with the understanding that neither the author nor the publisher is held responsible for the results accrued from the advice in this book.

WHY THIS BOOK

As a Chartered Accountant with over 14 years of experience, I have worked with countless startups, helping them navigate the intricate maze of **compliance** and **tax planning**.

One of the most common challenges faced by entrepreneurs is the complexity of understanding the various laws, taxes, and regulations that govern their businesses.

Many startups tend to neglect these aspects and often feel that these are secondary to their business operations or that they can address them later when the business grows.

Unfortunately, this can lead to **unforeseen penalties, missed tax-saving opportunities**, and a **lack of financial clarity**, all of which can hinder a startup's growth. This book is a response to that mindset.

This book was created to bridge that gap. **"Taxation Essentials and Compliance for Startups"** is your **go-to guide** for understanding and managing the crucial aspects of compliance and taxation from the **ground up**.

It's not just a theoretical approach; it's a practical, easy-to-understand, and actionable blueprint that will help entrepreneurs like you lay a strong financial and legal foundation for your startup.

The goal of this book is not to overwhelm you with technicalities but to **empower** you with the knowledge and tools you need to avoid common mistakes, ensure **legal compliance**, and leverage **tax-saving strategies** to enhance profitability and growth.

WHAT WILL YOU FIND INSIDE?

Inside this book, you will find **clear, practical guidance** on topics such as:

- **Business Structures and Taxation**: Understanding which business structure (Sole Proprietorship, Private Limited Company, LLP) is right for you and its impact on taxes and compliance.

- **The Importance of Compliance**: How to ensure your startup adheres to regulatory requirements and avoids penalties.

- **Tax Planning and Saving Strategies**: Actionable insights into how startups can save taxes, claim deductions, and optimize their tax liabilities.

- **Navigating GST**: Everything you need to know about GST, from registration to filing returns, ensuring your business remains compliant.

- **Employee Taxes and Benefits**: How to handle payroll taxes, Provident Fund (PF), Employee State Insurance (ESI), and other labor law compliances.

- **Government Schemes and Financial Aid**: How startups can benefit from government schemes such as **Startup India** and other tax benefits available to them.

- **Real-life Case Studies**: Practical examples from small and large businesses showing how strategic tax planning and compliance helped them grow.

You will also find **step-by-step instructions, tips**, and **tools** that will allow you to make better financial and business decisions. The book is filled with **actionable steps** so you can apply the concepts right away to your startup.

Who Should Read This Book?

This book is a must-read for:

- **Aspiring Entrepreneurs**: If you are looking to start a business or are in the early stages of your entrepreneurial journey, this book will help you lay the foundation for long-term success by ensuring your business is compliant from the start.

- **Small and Medium-Sized Enterprises (SMEs)**: If you are running a small business and want to streamline your tax processes, improve financial planning, and ensure compliance with Indian regulations, this book is for you.

- **Startup Founders and Co-founders**: Entrepreneurs in the startup ecosystem will find this book invaluable for navigating the complexities of **business registration, GST**, and **tax-saving schemes**.

- **Business Owners in Tier 2 and Tier 3 Cities**: Startups in smaller cities often face different challenges when it comes to compliance and taxation. This book addresses those challenges in a clear, actionable manner.

- **Financial Professionals and Aspiring CAs**: If you're a financial consultant, an accountant, or someone looking to gain deeper insight into startup tax and compliance strategies, this book will serve as a comprehensive resource.

Whether you are **just starting out** or have already begun your entrepreneurial journey, this book is designed to guide you through the **essential steps of managing taxes, staying compliant**, and **planning for growth**.

I hope this book provides the knowledge, confidence, and tools you need to build a **strong, sustainable foundation** for your startup. By taking the right steps now, you can save yourself from unnecessary hurdles down the road and ensure your business thrives in the long run.

Remember, getting it right from the start is the key to long-term success.

Welcome to your journey of **smart tax planning** and **strategic business growth**.

CA Megha Jain

Founder and Author

J Megha & Co.

TABLE OF CONTENTS

ABOUT THE AUTHOR 

CA Megha Jain is a highly experienced and dedicated Chartered Accountant (CA) with over **14 years of expertise** in the fields of **taxation, compliance, auditing**, and **startup advisory services**. With a proven track record in helping startups, small businesses, and established organizations navigate the complex world of taxation and business regulations, she has earned a reputation for her commitment to delivering clear, actionable, and effective solutions.

Her **passion for empowering startups** and entrepreneurs to thrive in a competitive business environment has driven her to specialize in **business registrations, tax planning**, and **compliance management**. She is known for her practical and client-focused approach, using her deep knowledge of Indian tax laws to help businesses save taxes, maximize growth, and ensure legal compliance.

CA Megha Jain works closely with **startups** across a wide range of industries, assisting them with

- **Company Formation,**

- **Tax Planning & Maximising Benefits,**

- **Stay Compliant with Government Regulations**

- **Strategic Advice**

- **And Many more...**

With her **hands-on expertise** and thorough understanding of the unique challenges faced by entrepreneurs, she provides customized solutions that are both cost-effective and efficient.

Educational Background:

CA Megha Jain holds a degree in Commerce from Kurukshetra University and is a member of the Institute of Chartered Accountants of India (ICAI) and a member of the Institute of Company Secretary of India (ICSI). Additionally, CA Megha Jain has completed various specialized diploma & certification courses in Various Taxation, Forensic Accounting & Fraud Detection, Information System Audit, and Banking Audits, etc.

Currently, Megha Jain is the founder of J Megha & Co., a Chartered Accountant Firm that was established in 2018 (Deemed 2012) in the heart of Bengaluru, India.

Publications and Speaking Engagements:

Beyond her professional work, CA Megha Jain is also an active speaker and educator, regularly conducting workshops and seminars to spread awareness about the importance of financial planning and tax compliance. She firmly believes that a **strong financial foundation** and a commitment to **legal compliance** are the keys to long-term business success.

This book is the culmination of her years of experience, offering valuable insights to startups on **tax planning**, **compliance**, and strategies for **growth and savings**. By sharing her knowledge, CA Megha Jain aims to empower entrepreneurs and business owners to make informed decisions, avoid common pitfalls, and set their businesses on the path to success.

PREFACE

Starting a business is an exciting and often exhilarating journey, filled with innovation, creativity, and the desire to bring something new to the world. However, alongside these exciting aspects, several critical elements cannot be ignored. One of the most crucial aspects is ensuring that your business complies with **taxation laws** and **regulations** while also strategically planning your finances to foster growth and maximize savings.

ACKNOWLEDGEMENTS 

Writing this book has been an incredible journey, and it would not have been possible without the support, encouragement, and inspiration of many individuals. I want to take this opportunity to express my heartfelt gratitude to all those who have contributed to the creation of this book.

1. My Family

I want to thank **my parents, Mrs. Usha Jain & Mr. Sanjay Jain**, whose sacrifices, unwavering love, and support have been the foundation of my journey. They have always believed in my dreams, even when circumstances were difficult. Despite facing many constraints, they prioritized my education and did everything in their power to ensure that I received the best opportunities to succeed. The values they instilled in me—resilience, determination, and the importance of education—have been the driving force behind my professional success.

To my **husband, Mr. Punith Jain (Er.)**, thank you for your patience and understanding during the countless hours spent working on this book. Your love and support have been my greatest motivators.

To my **two-year-old child, Mstr. Anay Jain**, though so young, your love and joy are a constant reminder of what truly matters. Even though you are still learning to talk, your smile, laughter, and pure presence have been a source of unspoken motivation. While I may have sacrificed time with you at times, every moment with you has been invaluable, and I am thankful for your patience as I balanced my professional goals with motherhood.

I look forward to sharing my journey with you as you grow.

To my **brother, Mr. Ankush Jain (IIT)**, whose unwavering support has been a constant in my life. Though younger than me, he has always taken on the role of a guiding figure, showing responsibility and strength beyond his years. Through every challenge and triumph, he has stood by me, and for that, I am eternally grateful. His belief in me has made all the difference in this journey.

To my younger brother, **Mr. Mohit Jain (CA)**, whose constant presence in my life has been a source of both challenge and strength. In times of hardship, he has been a pillar of support, offering encouragement and loyalty, even when words were few.

To my **parent**s-in-law, Mrs. Tharadevi & Mr. Ashok Kumar Jain, and especially my mother-in-law, During the difficult times when my mother-in-law was battling cancer, my in-laws showed immense patience and understanding as I could not always be there by her side due to my professional commitments.

They respected my passion and the dedication I had toward my work, even when it meant that I was physically distant. Their compassion and unwavering support during these challenging times meant the world to me, and I could not have asked for a better understanding and supportive parents-in-law.

2. **Mr. Gaurav Arora (My Mentor)**

A special thank you goes to **Mr. Gaurav Arora**, my **mentor**, whose guidance and invaluable advice have played a crucial role in shaping my professional journey. His insights and mentorship have not only broadened my understanding of business and taxation but have also inspired me to share this knowledge with others through this book. His belief in my vision has been a constant source of motivation.

3. **My Colleagues and My Team at J Megha & Co.**

My heartfelt appreciation goes to my colleagues and My office Team, who stepped up and shouldered additional responsibilities during my absence from the office. Their dedication and willingness to go the extra mile allowed me to focus on this book without compromising on professional commitments.

4. **My Clients and my Professional Brothers and Sisters**

A heartfelt thank you to the **entrepreneurs, clients, startups, and professional associates** I have had the privilege of working with over the years. Your real-world challenges, questions, and feedback have been invaluable in shaping the content of this book. Your stories of success, struggle, and resilience are the foundation of the practical advice shared within these pages. Thank you for trusting me. I hope this book continues to provide value to all of you as you navigate your entrepreneurial paths.

Finally, I would like to thank the **readers** of this book. Your decision to pick up this book and engage with the content is a step towards building a stronger, more sustainable business. I sincerely hope that the knowledge shared here helps you unlock the potential of your startup, save taxes, and achieve long-term success. It is because of your trust in my work that this book exists, and I am deeply honored.

Thank you to everyone who has been part of this incredible journey. This book is as much yours as it is mine.

CA Megha Jain

Founder and Author

J Megha & Co.

CHAPTER 1

INTRODUCTION

Starting a business is an exciting journey, but it also comes with numerous legal, financial, and operational challenges for entrepreneurs. In India, the startup ecosystem has grown tremendously in the last few years, with the government creating a favorable environment for innovation. Still, entrepreneurs often face difficulties when it comes to navigating the complex maze of tax regulations, compliance requirements, and government schemes due to the complexity of the Indian legal and financial framework.

As a practicing Chartered Accountant, I have worked with numerous startups, helping them manage registrations, comply with tax laws, and take full advantage of tax-saving opportunities. I've seen the pitfalls that startups can encounter if they don't understand the basics of registrations, compliances, and taxation.

This book provides a comprehensive guide to help you navigate the essential processes required for setting up and growing your business in India. Whether you're a first-time entrepreneur or someone looking to streamline your business operations, this book will provide the knowledge and tools you need to save costs, reduce taxes, and comply with all regulations.

In this guide, we'll cover everything you need to know—from choosing the right legal structure for your startup to managing taxes efficiently to raising capital and expanding your business.

The Importance of Getting It Right from the Start

Starting a business is no small feat. Every decision you make in the early stages has the potential to shape your company's future. One of the most critical aspects to get right at the outset is the **legal and financial framework** within which your business will operate. Whether you are a sole proprietor, a partnership, or have incorporated as a private limited company, your initial setup influences several aspects of your business, including:

- **Legal Liability**: The structure of your business determines your personal liability. For instance, a **sole proprietorship** exposes your personal assets to risk, while a **private limited company** can provide limited liability protection.

- **Taxation**: The way you register your business impacts the taxes you pay. Different business structures have distinct tax implications. For example, certain small businesses in India may qualify for tax exemptions under the **Startup India Scheme**, reducing the overall tax burden.

- **Financial Management**: Ensuring that you have the correct accounting system in place and keeping track of business expenses, revenues, and taxes right from day one can prevent major headaches in the future.

The key takeaway here is that a lack of attention to detail in the early stages of a startup can lead to legal issues, financial complications, and unnecessary tax liabilities that could easily have been avoided. Setting the right foundation through compliance, registration, and tax planning can **save time, money, and effort in the long run**, allowing you to focus on what matters most—growing your business.

How This Book Will Help Startups

This book serves as a comprehensive guide to navigating the complexities that come with starting and scaling a business in India. As an entrepreneur, it's easy to get bogged down by operational tasks, product development, and marketing, while legal and compliance issues may often take a backseat.

However, these aspects are just as crucial to the success of your startup. Here's how this book will help:

1. Step-by-step guidance on Legal Compliance

Understanding the regulatory landscape is often one of the most daunting aspects of running a business. This book will provide you with clear instructions on **how to register your business, file taxes**, and stay compliant with **GST** and **labor laws**. It will walk you through the process of setting up your business structure, ensuring that you understand what's required for each step, from business registration to post-incorporation compliance.

2. Taxation Tips for Startups

One of the biggest hurdles for startups is the tax burden. Whether it's **income tax**, **GST**, or **tax deductions**, businesses often struggle to make sense of tax regulations. This book will highlight the various **tax-saving strategies**, exemptions, and benefits available to startups, including **Startup India**, **MSME**, and other government initiatives. By understanding the available tax benefits, you can optimize your tax strategy and reduce unnecessary liabilities.

3. Cost-Saving Strategies and Financial Planning

Managing startup finances efficiently is key to survival. This book will offer insights on managing costs, setting up an **effective accounting system**, and ensuring **cash flow management** to help your business grow. Additionally, it will teach you how to streamline your operations to save money on administrative and operational costs.

4. Scaling and Growth Strategies

Once your startup is compliant and cost-efficient, it's time to focus on growth. This book will provide actionable insights into **scaling your business**, exploring funding options, and building a **brand presence**. By following these strategies, your business will be ready to scale both locally and nationally.

5. Case Studies and Real-world Examples

The book features several **real-life case studies** of startups that have successfully navigated the complexities of compliance and taxation. By learning from the success stories of others, you can apply their lessons to your own business. These case studies will also provide insights into common mistakes to avoid.

Why Compliance Is Critical for Growth and Tax Savings

Many entrepreneurs overlook the importance of compliance and tax management, assuming that it's something to deal with once their business becomes established. However, in reality, ensuring compliance from day one is **critical for the future growth** of your business. Here's why:

1. Avoiding Legal and Financial Penalties

Failure to comply with tax laws and business regulations can result in **fines**, **penalties**, and, in some cases, **closure orders**. For example, non-compliance with GST regulations can lead to hefty fines, while failing to maintain proper accounting records can result in penalties. By staying compliant, you can avoid these costly mistakes that can negatively affect your startup's reputation and financial stability.

2. Access to Tax Benefits and Exemptions

India offers several tax exemptions and benefits specifically designed for startups, such as the **Startup India Scheme, Section 80-IAC** tax deductions for businesses in specified regions, and exemptions for new

MSMEs. Startups that are **tax-compliant** can avail of these benefits, allowing them to reinvest more funds into their operations, scale faster, and grow sustainably. By failing to stay compliant, startups may miss out on these valuable tax-saving opportunities.

3. Building Credibility and Trust

Startups that maintain compliance with all relevant laws and regulations build credibility with investors, customers, and other stakeholders. This trust can be the difference between securing **funding** or **partnerships** and being passed over for someone else. Investors, for example, will not back a business that hasn't demonstrated strong compliance practices, as it presents unnecessary risks.

4. Business Sustainability and Longevity

Sustainability isn't just about being environmentally conscious; it's also about creating a stable financial and legal structure that will allow your business to last for years. Ensuring compliance with local laws, tax regulations, and other industry-specific requirements is crucial for the long-term viability of your startup. Building a solid legal and financial foundation will allow your business to weather economic challenges, regulatory changes, and market shifts more effectively.

5. Improved Operational Efficiency

Compliance often requires that you put systems in place to track finances, record transactions, and ensure tax filings are timely. These systems help improve your operational efficiency, ensuring that your business runs smoothly, stays organized, and avoids legal disputes down the road.

Conclusion: Setting the Stage for Success

As you can see, compliance isn't just about "doing things right" for the sake of following the law. It's about building a **solid foundation** for your startup to grow and scale successfully. This book is designed to help you navigate this crucial aspect of business management. By ensuring your startup is tax-compliant, legally structured, and financially disciplined from the beginning, you can focus on what matters most—**growing your business and achieving your entrepreneurial dreams**.

Through this guide, you'll learn the various steps to register your business, meet tax requirements, file necessary returns, and develop financial strategies that can help you grow your startup while remaining compliant with Indian laws.

In the next chapters, we'll dive deeper into the practical steps you need to take, from choosing the right business structure to understanding tax-saving techniques and creating a sustainable financial plan. So, let's get started on building your startup's future—**the right way from day one**.

CHAPTER 2

20 COMMON MYTHS VS. REALITY ABOUT COMPLIANCE AND TAXATION FOR STARTUPS

There are a few **common myths** that startup founders often believe when it comes to **compliance** and **taxation**. Let's address these myths to give a more complete picture of the misconceptions startups may have and help you avoid them:

Myth 1: "I don't know the correct path to do business."

- **Reality**: It's common to feel uncertain when starting a business, but there is a clear path if you break it down into manageable steps. With proper research, mentorship, and planning, you can gain clarity. Starting with understanding your industry, identifying your target market, creating a solid business plan, and seeking advice from experts or advisors can provide guidance.

There are also many resources, from government programs to online courses, that can help you navigate the process. Remember, every successful business starts with learning and adapting—you're not alone in this journey.

Myth 2: "Being a newly incorporated entity, I need not follow all compliances."

- **Reality:** Registering your business is just the first step. Compliance is an **ongoing process**. Starting a new business doesn't exempt you from compliance requirements. In fact, newly incorporated companies are subject to several legal obligations right from the beginning.

These include registering for taxes, maintaining proper financial records, filing annual returns, holding regular board meetings, and complying with labor and environmental laws. Failing to adhere to these can result in penalties, legal issues, or even the dissolution of your company. It's crucial to understand and fulfill all regulatory requirements to ensure your business operates smoothly and legally from day one.

Myth 3: "Compliance Is Too Expensive and Complicated for Startups."

Or "There is a lot of Compliance, which is Expensive and Complicated, so I should not run a business in India."

Or "I do not have time and money to invest in the Compliances."

- **Reality**: While it may seem like an added burden, investing time and money in compliance is essential for the long-term success of your business. The costs of non-compliance are much higher in the long run. Penalties, fines, and potential legal battles can drain your startup's resources, far outweighing the initial costs of setting up the right compliance structures.

In fact, with the help of a good chartered accountant or tax advisor, the process can be streamlined and made much more affordable than expected.

Myth 4: "A Sole Proprietorship Is the Simplest and Cheapest Option."

Or "There is no compliance cost to have a Sole Proprietorship firm; hence, we are saving huge money."

- **Reality**: While a **sole proprietorship** might seem like an easy and inexpensive way to start a business, it comes with **personal liability risks** that can affect your personal assets. Moreover, certain tax benefits and funding options might not be available for sole proprietorships.

  A **Private Limited Company** or **Limited Liability Partnership (LLP)** can offer better protection for your personal assets, gain lower tax rates, provide access to more funding options, and enhance your business's credibility. Also, It is beneficial for those who want to take their business to the next generation.

Myth 5: "Compliance Is Just About Filing Income Tax Returns (ITRs)."

- **Reality**: Compliance extends far beyond **filing tax returns**. It also involves registering your business with the appropriate authorities, adhering to **labor laws**, ensuring **GST registration**, maintaining proper **financial records**, conducting **annual audits**, and **filing required forms** with relevant government agencies.

Tax returns are just one part of the larger compliance landscape. Overlooking other obligations can lead to missed deadlines or regulatory violations.

Myth 6: "Only Large Businesses Need to Worry About Tax Planning."

- **Reality**: **Tax planning is equally important for startups**, regardless of their size. Small businesses may feel that they don't generate enough income to require sophisticated tax planning, but in reality, tax-saving strategies can have a huge impact on a startup's bottom line.

Entrepreneurs should take full advantage of tax benefits available to them, such as **tax deductions for expenses, deductions for capital investments**, and **government schemes** designed specifically for startups.

Failing to plan effectively can lead to unnecessary tax liabilities that could have been minimized.

Myth 7: "I Can Do Everything Myself; I Don't Need a Tax Advisor or Chartered Accountant."

Or "I have sufficient knowledge to file my ITR and GST Return, I can do it myself."

- **Reality**: While it's possible to learn the basics of taxes and compliance on your own, having a **qualified tax advisor** or **chartered accountant** can save your startup **time, money, and effort**.

Navigating the complex Indian taxation and compliance system can be overwhelming.

A professional can help you stay updated with regulatory changes, ensure you're optimizing your tax strategy, and avoid costly mistakes. Having expert guidance can prevent errors in filings, missed deadlines, or underreporting, all of which can lead to penalties or lost opportunities for tax savings.

Myth 8: "It doesn't matter how I am earning; my tax liability should not increase every year."

- **Reality:** Your tax liability can increase if your income rises, even if the source of your earnings remains the same. As your business grows or you earn more, tax rates and applicable thresholds can change. This is because tax systems are designed to scale with income.

However, you can manage and minimize your tax burden through tax planning, deductions, and credits available for your business structure. It's important to stay informed and work with a tax professional to optimize your liabilities and ensure you're not paying more than necessary.

Myth 9: "All Documentation and Tax Filings Can Be Done at the End of the Year."

- **Reality**: Procrastination can cost startups a lot. Many entrepreneurs assume that they can defer tax filings until the end of the financial year, but **filing at the last minute** can lead to **missed deductions**, **penalties**, or **errors**.

In reality, **quarterly filings** for **GST**, **income tax** (if applicable), and other compliance requirements should be made **periodically** throughout the year.

This proactive approach will ensure that you avoid **late fees** and **interest charges** and keep your books in order.

Myth 10: "I Don't Need to Worry About GST Until My Revenue Crosses a Certain Threshold."

Or "There is no benefit of registering under GST; rather, I need to bear registration & return filing costs."

- **Reality**: In India, **GST registration** is mandatory for businesses with a turnover above a certain threshold.

However, even if your turnover doesn't cross that threshold, you may **voluntarily register for GST** if it benefits your business.

For example, registering for GST allows businesses to claim **input tax credits** (ITC) on the GST paid on purchases, thereby reducing overall costs.

Additionally, if you plan to scale your business, getting registered early helps in building a good **compliance track record** and may be seen as a **sign of credibility** when you approach investors or partners.

Myth 11: **"I am fed up with regular changes in law."**

- **Reality**: While it's true that laws and regulations can change frequently, these updates are often designed to improve business practices, protect consumers, and support economic growth. Staying updated with these changes ensures that your business remains compliant and avoids penalties.

Adapting to legal changes can also provide opportunities to streamline operations, take advantage of new incentives, or implement better practices.

Rather than seeing it as a hassle, view it as a way to future-proof your business and stay competitive in an evolving market.

Myth 12: "The Indian government is charging a lot of taxes from us but not giving any benefits."

- **Reality**: While taxes may seem high, they fund essential public services like infrastructure, healthcare, education, and national defense, all of which benefit businesses and citizens alike. The government also offers numerous incentives, subsidies, and schemes, especially for startups and small businesses, such as tax deductions, GST exemptions, and financial support programs.

Additionally, the tax system ensures social welfare benefits like pensions, healthcare programs, and subsidies for various sectors. It's important to understand the broader role taxes play in society and explore available benefits to maximize the support for your business.

Myth 13: "My CA is charging very high while I am paying a lot of taxes, and my friend can do it for a lower price."

- **Reality**: While it might seem like your CA is charging more, the value they bring goes beyond just filing taxes. A good CA helps you with proper tax planning, ensures compliance with ever-changing laws, and identifies deductions or exemptions you may not be aware of.

Their expertise can save you money in the long run by optimizing your tax strategy. Your friend's lower-priced option may not offer the same level of professional advice or may miss key opportunities, leading to future complications or penalties. Investing in a qualified CA can ultimately help you save more and avoid costly mistakes.

Myth 14: "My friend is not a CA, but he took my financials to another CA at a very low cost."

- **Reality**: While it may seem like a good deal, having a non-CA handle your financials can be risky. A qualified CA not only ensures that your financial statements comply with legal standards but also provides valuable insights into tax planning and financial strategies.

Using a lower-cost or unqualified professional may result in errors, missed deductions, or even legal complications down the line. It's important to invest in experienced professionals to safeguard your business's financial health and avoid potential penalties or audits.

Myth 15: "Why should I comply with a lot of things when my vendor, customer, or friend with the same business isn't following all compliances?"

- **Reality**: Just because others are not complying doesn't mean it's safe or wise to follow suit. Non-compliance can lead to serious legal consequences, fines, or even the closure of your business. It's essential to follow all regulations to protect your business, reputation, and personal assets. In the long run, staying compliant ensures smooth operations, builds trust with clients and investors, and positions your business for sustainable growth. Cutting corners now could result in much bigger problems later.

Myth 16: "I got a notice from the department; it means my CA or accountant has not done proper work or done something wrong."

- **Reality**: Receiving a notice from the department doesn't necessarily mean that your CA or accountant has made a mistake. Notices can be triggered for a variety of reasons, such as discrepancies, missed deadlines, or routine audits. Sometimes, it could be due to errors in the system or clerical issues.

A qualified CA will help you address the notice by reviewing the details and providing the necessary documentation or corrections. It's important to stay calm and work with your professional to resolve any issues rather than assuming blame immediately.

Myth 17: "My CA always gives me a calculation to pay TDS, advance tax, or professional tax and keeps threatening that if I don't pay, I'll be in trouble."

- **Reality**: What your CA is doing is helping you stay compliant with the law and avoid penalties. Taxes like TDS, advance tax, and professional tax are mandatory and need to be paid on time to avoid interest, fines, or legal issues.

While it may feel like a threat, it's actually sound advice to ensure you meet your tax obligations. Paying taxes on time not only keeps you legally safe but also helps your business avoid unnecessary complications in the future. Proper tax planning and timely payments are part of running a responsible business.

Myth 18: "There are a lot of online portals offering services at a lower cost, so I can assign my tasks to them."

- **Reality**: While online portals may seem like a cheaper option, they often lack the personalized service and expertise that a qualified professional can offer. The risk of errors, miscommunication, or non-compliance is higher with cheaper, impersonal services.

These platforms might not fully understand your business's unique needs or local regulations. Investing in a trusted, experienced professional ensures accuracy, compliance, and long-term stability for your business, preventing costly mistakes down the road.

Quality service often outweighs cost savings when it comes to important tasks like tax filings or financial planning.

Myth 19: "Why should I give a lot of personal, work, and internal documents to my CA?"

- **Reality**: Providing your CA with personal, work, and internal documents is essential for them to accurately understand your financial situation and ensure compliance with tax laws. These documents help them assess your business structure, track your income and expenses, and identify potential deductions or tax-saving opportunities. A CA's role is to protect your financial interests and to do that effectively, they need complete information. Sharing the necessary documents ensures proper planning and avoids errors, audits, or penalties in the future. It's a step towards safeguarding your business and personal financial health.

Myth 20: "My CA will handle everything, so I don't need to understand the financial side of my business."

- **Reality**: While a CA is critical for advising and ensuring compliance, as a business owner, you need to have a basic understanding of your financials.

Knowledge of your cash flow, profit margins, and tax obligations helps you make informed decisions and better collaborate with your CA.

Conclusion: Clearing the Air on Myths

The myths mentioned above can often prevent startups from fully understanding the importance of compliance and taxation.

By debunking these myths, entrepreneurs can make **informed decisions** that will help their business grow smoothly, avoid legal issues, and take full advantage of available opportunities.

The reality is that **taxation and compliance are not just obligations—** they are tools that can significantly enhance the **financial health** and **sustainability** of a startup.

Consulting with professionals like **Chartered Accountants** and using technology to stay compliant can save you time, reduce risks, and ensure your startup grows without any legal or financial hurdles.

UNDERSTANDING STARTUPS AND THEIR LEGAL STRUCTURE

3.1 What is a Startup?

Not all businesses are startups, but all startups are businesses. A **business** is any organization or entity that provides goods or services to customers with the goal of making a profit. It can be small, large, established, or in a steady state of growth. A **startup**, on the other hand, is a business that is in the early stages of development, typically focused on innovation, scalability, and high growth potential.

While every startup is a business, it differs in its initial focus on innovation, market disruption, and rapid scaling, which sets it apart from traditional businesses that may not have such high-risk, high-reward goals.

In India, the term "startup" is more than just a buzzword. A startup is defined by the Indian government under the **Startup India** initiative as an entity that is less than 10 years old, has an annual turnover of less than ₹100 crores, and is engaged in innovative activities in terms of development or improvement of products, services, or processes.

Startups are unique because they tend to be agile, innovative, and often tech-driven. However, before diving into operations, it's crucial to understand the legal structure of your startup.

The legal structure will not only impact your day-to-day operations but also determine your tax liabilities, ownership, and the funding options available.

Starting a business in India is not just about having a good idea or product; it's about setting the right foundation. The first crucial step is deciding on the legal structure of your business. The structure you choose will determine your liability, tax obligations, and the overall operations of the company.

3.2 Different Types of Business Structures

1. **Sole Proprietorship:**

   o **Overview:** A sole proprietorship is the simplest form of business structure where an individual operates the business alone and assumes all the risks and responsibilities for the business. It's quick to set up but offers no protection for personal assets.

   o **Advantages:** Simple to set up, low compliance burden, complete control over decision-making.

   o **Disadvantages:** Unlimited liability, limited scalability, and credibility issues.

2. **Partnership:**

- o   **Overview:** A partnership involves two or more individuals who share profits, losses, and responsibilities. It's suitable for businesses where owners want to share responsibilities but still maintain a simple structure.

- o   **Advantages:** More capital can be raised compared to a sole proprietorship, sharing of responsibilities.

- o   **Disadvantages:** Unlimited liability, potential conflicts between partners.

3. **Limited Liability Partnership (LLP):**

- o   **Overview:** LLP is a hybrid between a partnership and a private limited company. Partners have limited liability, which means their personal assets are protected. This is a popular choice for startups due to its flexibility and legal protection.

- o   **Advantages:** Limited liability for partners, flexibility in internal management, and fewer compliances.

- o   **Disadvantages:** It may not be as credible as a private limited company in the eyes of investors.

4. **Private Limited Company:**

- o   **Overview:** A private limited company is a separate legal entity from its owners (shareholders). It offers limited liability, and shares can be transferred to investors or partners.

A Private Limited Company is the most preferred business structure for startups. It's also ideal for raising capital from investors.

- **Advantages:** Limited liability, ease of raising capital, and credibility.

- **Disadvantages:** Higher regulatory burden and compliance costs.

5. **Public Limited Company:**

- **Overview:** A public limited company can raise capital from the general public by issuing shares, which are listed on the stock exchange. However, the regulatory requirements are complex, making it less suitable for early-stage startups. It is subject to stringent regulations from SEBI and MCA.

- **Advantages:** Ability to raise large sums of capital and high credibility.

- **Disadvantages:** Heavy regulatory burden and cost of compliance.

3.3 Choosing the Right Firm Name is also essential

Your firm's name is more than just a label—it reflects your identity, values, and the nature of your business.

A thoughtfully chosen name can enhance brand recall, convey professionalism, and align with your long-term vision. It should also be compliant with naming guidelines under the chosen business structure, whether it's a Sole Proprietorship, LLP, or Private Limited Company.

A strong, meaningful name lays the foundation for credibility and future growth.

3.4 Key Questions to Ask Before Choosing the Right Business Structure:

Choosing the right business structure is a critical decision for any startup. Here are some key questions to ask yourself before making this choice:

1. **What are my liability concerns?**

   o   Am I willing to take on personal liability for business debts and obligations, or do I want to limit my personal exposure?

2. **What is my long-term vision for the business?**

   o   Do I plan to grow and scale quickly, or is this a small, manageable operation? Will I need to raise funds from investors?

3. **How much control do I want over decision-making?**

   o   Do I want full control over all decisions, or would I prefer to have partners or shareholders involved in the business?

4. **What are my tax considerations?**

- What tax advantages or disadvantages might each structure offer? How will it affect my personal taxes and the company's tax obligations?

5. **What is my capital requirement?**

   - How much capital will I need to start the business, and do I intend to raise funds from outside investors?

6. **What is the risk of my business?**

   - How risky is my business, and do I need to protect myself from potential lawsuits or debts?

7. **How easy is it to transfer ownership or exit?**

   - In the event that I want to sell my business or pass it on, how easy is it to transfer ownership or exit from the structure?

8. **What are the compliance and regulatory requirements?**

   - How much paperwork, reporting, and compliance will be required under different structures?

9. **Number of owners or partners involved**

   - How many numbers of owners or partners will be involved or required?

Answering these questions will help you evaluate which business structure (e.g., Sole Proprietorship, Partnership, Private Limited Company, LLP, etc.) best suits your needs and goals.

For most early-stage startups, **Private Limited Company** and **Limited Liability Partnership (LLP)** are the most commonly chosen structures and are recommended for their scalability and liability protection. Both offer limited liability, which is crucial for protecting personal assets.

CHAPTER 4

GETTING STARTED: KEY REGISTRATIONS FOR YOUR STARTUP

Once you've decided on your business structure, the next step is to complete all necessary registrations. Starting a business in India requires navigating a variety of legal processes.

These processes ensure that your business complies with all necessary regulations, pays taxes on time, and is eligible for various government incentives.

This chapter covers the key registrations your startup needs in order to function legally and efficiently.

4.1 Company Registration (ROC Filing)

For startups looking to incorporate as a Private Limited Company, Limited Liability Partnership (LLP), or another corporate structure, you'll need to register with the Ministry of Corporate Affairs (MCA). The registration process involves:

- **Name Approval:** You must choose a unique name for your company.

- File for Digital Signature Certificates (DSC).

- **Filing Documents:** Submit the memorandum and articles of association, along with the director's details and business address.

- **Incorporation Certificate:** Once registered, you will receive the Certificate of Incorporation, which is necessary to conduct business operations legally in India.

4.2 GST Registration

The Goods and Services Tax (GST) is a value-added tax levied on the supply of goods and services. As a business owner, you must register for GST if:

- Your annual turnover exceeds the prescribed limit set by the government (which may vary depending on the type of business and its location).

- You are providing services or selling products that are taxable under GST.

Even if you are not required to register under the threshold limit, voluntary registration is advisable to avail benefits such as:

- Input tax credit (ITC) on purchases

- Increased credibility with customers and suppliers

Types of GST Registration:

- **Regular Scheme:** Most businesses with turnover exceeding the limit must register under the regular scheme.

- **Composition Scheme:** A simplified scheme for small businesses with turnover under ₹1.5 crores, offering lower tax rates and reduced compliance burden.

4.3 PAN and TAN Registration

- **PAN (Permanent Account Number):** PAN is required for all businesses and acts as a tax identifier, which is issued by the Income Tax Department. PAN is essential for all financial transactions, including opening a bank account and filing taxes.

- **TAN (Tax Deduction and Collection Account Number):** If your business is liable to deduct tax at source (TDS) from salaries, payments to contractors, payments to professionals, or rent, you need to apply for TAN.

4.4 Other Essential Registrations

4.4.1 Professional Tax (PT)

Professional Tax is applicable in certain states. If your business operates in such a state, you need to register and deduct PT from employee salaries. The rate and process differ across states. If you are hiring employees, you need to comply with the local professional tax laws.

4.4.2   Provident Fund (PF)

The Employees' Provident Fund (EPF) is a social security scheme that aims to provide financial security to employees after retirement. Both the employer and the employee contribute to the EPF.

- **Applicability**: It applies to all establishments employing 20 or more employees. It is mandatory for employees earning a basic salary of up to ₹15,000 per month.

- **Registration**: Employers must register with the **Employees' Provident Fund Organisation (EPFO)** and ensure that the contributions are made within the prescribed due dates.

4.4.3 Employees' State Insurance (ESI)

The Employees' State Insurance (ESI) scheme is a health insurance scheme for employees to cover medical expenses, sickness benefits, and other social security benefits.

- **Applicability**: ESI is mandatory for employees earning a monthly wage of ₹21,000 or less (₹25,000 for employees with disabilities). ESI applies to factories, shops, and establishments with 10 or more employees.

- **Employer's Responsibility**: Employers must register their employees with the **Employees' State Insurance Corporation (ESIC)** and ensure that ESI contributions are paid regularly.

4.4.4 MSME Registration

Micro, Small, and Medium Enterprises (MSME) registration offers benefits like priority sector lending and government schemes, which are beneficial for startups.

4.4.5 Startup Registration

There are a lot of benefits available under the startup scheme launched by the Govt for those Startups who are registered with the Department for Promotion of Industry and Internal Trade (DPIIT), like 3 years tax exemption, seed funding, non-refundable govt grants, concession on ipr registration, ease of business, etc. to eligible businesses.

4.5 Special Registrations for Specific Industries:

4.5.1 FSSAI Registration (for Food Businesses)

If your startup operates in the food sector, obtaining a Food Safety and Standards Authority of India (FSSAI) license is essential.

4.5.2 Import Export Code (IEC)

If your startup is involved in import or export, you must apply for an IEC from the Directorate General of Foreign Trade (DGFT).

4.5.3 Intellectual Property (IP) Registrations

- **Trademark Registration**: If you want to protect your company name, logo, or brand identity, registering a trademark is essential.

- **Patent Registration**: If your startup has invented a new product or process, applying for a patent may be necessary to protect it.

- **Copyright Registration**: If you have original creative works (e.g., software, art, writing), registering copyrights ensures your intellectual property is protected.

4.5.4 Environmental and Safety Registrations (if your business impacts the environment or needs waste management)

4.5.5 Employment and Labor Registration

4.5.6 **Obtain Industry-Specific Licenses/Permits** (e.g., health, food, alcohol, finance, etc.)

4.5.7 **Obtain Health & Safety Permits** (if required, e.g., food safety or workplace safety)

4.5.8 **Register for Zoning Permits** (if operating a physical location, e.g., SEZ Zone, STP Zone)

Conclusion:

In conclusion, registering your startup with the necessary authorities is a critical step towards building a legal and compliant business in India. Each registration, from company incorporation to tax identification and industry-specific licenses, ensures that your business operates smoothly, meets regulatory requirements, and qualifies for government benefits.

By following these essential registration processes, you lay a solid foundation for your startup's growth and avoid future legal complications. It is important to stay informed and proactive about the various registrations required to keep your business legally sound and eligible for the benefits that can accelerate your success.

CHAPTER 5

TAXATION ESSENTIALS AND COMPLIANCES YOU NEED TO FOLLOW

After registration, ongoing compliance becomes the core of your business operations. Complying with regulations is a continuous process that every business must follow.

Non-compliance can result in hefty fines and legal consequences. Here are the key compliance requirements your startup must follow to stay legally protected.

5.1 Taxation Essentials

5.1.1 Income Tax Compliance

Startups must comply with the **Income Tax Act** and file their income tax returns (ITR) annually. Keeping track of income and expenses, paying advance tax, and maintaining proper records are critical.

Key compliance requirements include:

- **Advance Tax Payments:** Pay taxes quarterly if your tax liability exceeds ₹10,000 in a year.

- **Tax Audit:** Companies and LLPs must undergo a tax audit if their annual turnover exceeds ₹1 crore.

- **ITR Filing:** All businesses must file annual income tax returns under Section 139(1) of the Income Tax Act. The due date for filing income tax returns varies based on the type of business (individual, company, or LLP).

Applicable To: All types of businesses, including startups, are required to pay income tax on their annual profits.

Taxable Income: For a startup, the taxable income includes all income generated from the business minus any allowable deductions.

Tax Rates: The applicable income tax rate depends on the structure of the business (proprietorship, partnership, LLP, or company).

- **For Individual/Proprietorship**: The tax rates are progressive and depend on the income slab. For example, if income is less than ₹2.5 lakh, no tax is levied. Between ₹2.5 lakh and ₹5 lakh, the tax is 5%, and so on.

  - Tax Regimes: There are two tax regimes available for individuals:

    The New Regime (with no deductions and exemptions), and

    The Old Regime (which allows deductions like 80C, 80D, and exemptions such as HRA).

o   Basic Structure: Tax rates are progressive, meaning the more you earn, the higher the rate. Rates vary based on income levels, with higher taxes for those earning more than ₹10 lakh.

o   Senior Citizens: There are relaxed tax limits for senior citizens (aged 60 to 80) and super senior citizens (aged 80+), offering higher exemptions before tax kicks in.

o   Cess: A 4% Health and Education Cess is levied on the total tax payable.

However, they may benefit from the Presumptive Taxation Scheme under Section 44AD for businesses with turnover under ₹2 crore, where income is presumed to be 8% of turnover and no further details need to be filed.

- **For Companies**: In India, the income tax rate for domestic companies is typically **25%** for businesses with a turnover of less than ₹400 crore and **30%** for larger businesses. Additionally, companies can opt for the **new tax regime** (under section 115BAA), where they pay tax at a reduced rate of **22%** without claiming deductions.

- **Startup Tax Benefits**: The **Startup India Scheme** provides tax exemptions for eligible startups. If your business qualifies as a startup, you can benefit from a **3-year tax holiday** for any 3 consecutive years out of 10 years from the date of incorporation (provided you meet certain conditions).

Other Income Tax Essentials:

1. **Minimum Alternate Tax (MAT)**

    o   **MAT** is applicable to companies that pay taxes under regular provisions but whose book profits are higher than the tax payable under the regular income tax regime. The MAT rate is **15%** on book profits.

    o   MAT is intended to ensure that companies with high book profits but minimal taxable income still contribute to taxes.

2. **Capital Gains Tax:** When selling assets or shares, startups must consider capital gains tax, which depends on the holding period of the asset.

5.1.2 GST Compliance

GST is levied on goods and services and is paid by consumers but collected and remitted by businesses.

For businesses, it is essential to understand which goods and services are subject to GST, the applicable rate, and how to file returns.

GST is a critical compliance requirement for most businesses. GST returns must be filed monthly or quarterly, and they include:

GST returns:

- **GSTR-1:** Monthly Outward supply details.

- **GSTR-3B:** Monthly summary of inward and outward supplies, tax liability, and payments.

- **GSTR-9:** Annual return detailing total sales, purchases, and tax payments.

- **GSTR-9C:** GSTR-9C is a **Self – Certified Reconciliation Statement** required to be filed by every business that has a turnover exceeding ₹5 crore in a financial year. It is to be filed alongside the GSTR-9 **Annual Return**. This document is designed to ensure that the taxpayer's GST returns are accurately reconciled with the company's **audited financial statements**.

Ensure timely filing to avoid penalties and interest.

GST Payments: GST payments need to be made regularly, and startups must ensure that input tax credit (ITC) is properly utilized to reduce tax liabilities.

GST Exemptions: Startups in specific industries such as education, healthcare, or non-profit organizations may be eligible for GST exemptions.

GST Rates: The rate of GST depends on the nature of the product or service. There are multiple tax slabs:

- 5%, 12%, 18%, and 28%.

It's essential to understand whether your business is eligible for GST exemptions or whether you qualify for the Composition Scheme.

5.1.3 TDS Compliance

If your business makes payments subject to TDS (e.g., employee salaries, rent, contractors, professional fees), you need to:

- Deduct the correct amount of tax.

- **File TDS Returns:** File quarterly TDS returns (Form 24Q for salary, Form 26Q for others).

- **Deposit TDS on Time:** Deposit the deducted tax with the government within the prescribed deadlines.

- **Form 26AS:** This is a statement that shows the TDS deducted by the payer on your behalf. Ensure that this matches with your payments and the TDS returns filed by the deductor.

5.1.4 Professional Tax (PT)

Professional Tax (PT) is a state-level tax imposed on individuals earning an income through employment, profession, trade, or calling. It is deducted from the salaries of employees and paid to the state government.

Employers are responsible for deducting PT from the salaries of employees and remitting it to the state government within the prescribed due date.

5.1.5 Provident Fund (PF)

The Employees' Provident Fund (EPF) is a social security scheme that aims to provide financial security to employees after retirement. Both the employer and the employee contribute to the EPF.

- **Contribution**:

    Employee Contribution: 12% of basic salary + dearness allowance (which is deducted from their salary).

    Employer Contribution: 12% of basic salary + dearness allowance (Out of the employer's 12%, 3.67% is contributed to the EPF account, while the remaining 8.33% is contributed to the EPS (Employees' Pension Scheme).

5.1.6 Employees' State Insurance (ESI)

The Employees' State Insurance (ESI) scheme is a health insurance scheme for employees to cover medical expenses, sickness benefits, and other social security benefits.

- **Contribution**:

    Employee Contribution: 0.75% of gross salary.

    Employer Contribution: 3.25% of gross salary.

ESI contributions go toward providing various welfare benefits like medical care, sickness, and maternity benefits.

5.1.7 Corporate Social Responsibility (CSR)

Certain companies must also comply with CSR regulations, mandating them to contribute to social causes if they meet certain revenue criteria.

5.1.8 Labor Law Compliance: Ensure that you comply with labor laws regarding employee rights, salaries, and working conditions to avoid legal troubles.

5.1.9 Customs Duty: If your startup is importing goods for business purposes, you may need to pay customs duties. The rates vary depending on the type of goods being imported.

5.2 Accounting and Bookkeeping Requirements

Maintaining proper books of accounts is essential not only for tax compliance but also for making informed business decisions. Below are some key requirements for accounting and bookkeeping:

Accounting Standards

- **Indian Accounting Standards (Ind AS):** As a startup, it's essential to follow accounting standards set by the Ministry of Corporate Affairs (MCA). Private limited companies must follow Ind AS or Accounting Standards (AS) as applicable, while for smaller entities, simplified accounting norms may apply.

- **Audited Financial Statements:** Startups that are companies or LLPs are required to prepare audited financial statements. This includes the Balance Sheet, Profit & Loss Account, and Cash Flow Statement.

Bookkeeping Practices

- **Accrual Basis of Accounting:** According to Indian accounting rules, businesses must follow the accrual method of accounting, where revenue is recorded when earned, and expenses are recorded when incurred, regardless of when the cash transaction occurs.

- **Maintain Proper Books:** Entrepreneurs need to maintain detailed records for each transaction (sales, purchases, expenses, etc.). This includes maintaining:

  o Sales and purchase invoices

  o Receipts and payments

  o Bank statements

  o Payroll records

Use of Accounting Software

- It is highly recommended that you use accounting software such as Tally, Zoho Books, or QuickBooks to manage your books more efficiently.

- These tools can generate GST-compliant invoices, track TDS, generate financial statements, and make tax filing easier.

Audit Requirements

- As mentioned earlier, companies and LLPs with a turnover exceeding ₹1 crore are required to undergo an audit. The auditor must verify the financial statements and issue an audit report before the ITR filing deadline.

5.3 Statutory Audit and Annual Filings

Companies must undergo an **annual audit** by a practicing Chartered Accountant (CA). This ensures that financial statements are accurate and comply with accounting standards and the Companies Act 2013.

Along with the audit, you must file to ROC:

Annual Return Filing

- Private limited companies and LLPs must file a Financial Statement and an annual return with the Registrar of Companies (RoC) within 30 days & 60 days, respectively, from the end of the Annual General Meeting (AGM).

- For private limited companies, Form MGT-7 (Annual Return) and Form AOC-4 (Financial Statements) must be submitted.

Director's Report

- The director's report must be submitted annually. It must include a detailed account of the company's financial performance, corporate governance, and compliance with relevant laws.

Board Meetings and Resolutions

- A private limited company or LLP must hold board meetings at least once a year. The minutes of these meetings need to be documented properly.

- Shareholder Resolutions and Board Resolutions must be maintained and recorded.

Other Filings and Documentation

- Form DIR-12: Changes in directors (if any) must be filed with the RoC.

- Form CHG-1: For registering charges (if any) on the company's assets.

Common Tax Mistakes Startups Make and How to Avoid Them

Startups, especially those in the early stages, are often unaware of the nuances of tax laws, which can lead to costly mistakes. Here are common tax mistakes and tips to avoid them:

1. **Failing to Register for GST**: If your turnover exceeds the GST registration threshold, failure to register for GST can result in penalties. Ensure timely registration to avoid non-compliance.

2. **Not Keeping Proper Records**: Poor record-keeping leads to issues during audits and tax filing. Maintain thorough financial records, including receipts, invoices, and contracts.

3. **Incorrect Tax Deductions**: Many startups fail to maximize deductions available to them, such as those for R&D or capital expenditures. Consult a tax expert to ensure you're claiming all eligible deductions.

4. **Delaying Tax Filings**: Filing tax returns late leads to penalties and interest charges. Stay on top of deadlines and file returns on time.

5. **Underestimating Advance Tax Liability**: Failure to pay advance tax when required can lead to interest charges. Estimate your tax liability and pay in instalments.

Staying Compliant with Tax Laws

Tax laws are constantly evolving. As a startup, you must stay updated on changes that could impact your business. Here's how to stay on top of things:

- Monitor tax laws: Keep an eye on any changes in tax legislation that could affect your business. Governments often release updates on tax incentives, exemptions, and changes in rates, so it's important to follow them.

- Consult a tax professional: Tax laws can be complex and vary based on your business's location and industry. A qualified tax professional can help you understand the latest regulations and assist with filing your taxes accurately.

- Be aware of tax audits: Tax authorities can audit your business if they suspect discrepancies in your tax filings. Keep your records up to date, file returns accurately, and be prepared for audits if necessary.

Conclusion

Understanding taxation is vital for the success of your startup. By staying compliant with tax regulations, taking advantage of exemptions, and implementing sound tax planning strategies, your startup can minimize its tax burden and optimize cash flow. Whether you're just starting out or looking to scale, taking the time to understand the tax landscape will help you avoid pitfalls, maximize deductions, and focus on growing your business.

CHAPTER 6

COST SAVING AND TAX PLANNING STRATEGIES

As a startup, managing costs and optimizing tax planning are crucial components of achieving financial stability and long-term success. Effective cost-saving measures and tax planning strategies not only help startups maximize their profits but also create a solid foundation for sustainable growth. By carefully managing business expenses and taking advantage of available tax exemptions, deductions, and incentives, startups can keep their overheads low, allocate resources more efficiently, and make informed decisions about reinvesting profits back into the business.

In this chapter, we will discuss various cost-saving strategies across different business functions, as well as key tax planning techniques that can help startups minimize tax liabilities and maximize savings.

6.1 Cost-Saving Strategies for Startups

Cost management is one of the most critical aspects of running a successful startup. With limited resources, startups need to adopt strategies that will allow them to maintain control over their expenses while still providing value to their customers. Here are some cost-saving strategies to consider:

6.1.1 Optimizing Operational Costs

1. Outsource Non-Core Activities

   o Outsourcing non-core business functions such as accounting, payroll, IT services, and customer support can help reduce labor costs while still maintaining high service standards.

   o Outsourcing means you only pay for the services you need, and you don't have to invest in additional infrastructure or hire full-time staff.

2. Adopt Technology and Automation

   o Cloud-Based Tools: Implement cloud-based tools for accounting, project management, and communication (e.g., Trello, Slack, Zoho, QuickBooks, Google Workspace) to reduce costs related to physical infrastructure and streamline processes.

   o Automation Software: Use automation tools for repetitive tasks such as invoicing, email marketing, and social media management.

3. Negotiate with Vendors and Suppliers

- o Establish long-term relationships with your suppliers to negotiate better prices for goods and services. Ask for volume discounts or flexible payment terms to reduce cash flow pressure.

- o Regularly assess and compare vendor contracts to ensure you're getting the best deal. Also, consider alternative suppliers if they offer better pricing or quality.

4. Reduce Office Space Costs

- o Startups don't always need a physical office space, especially in the early stages. Consider co-working spaces or virtual offices to save on rent, utilities, and maintenance costs.

- o For businesses that require office space, adopting a hybrid work model (remote work with occasional in-office meetings) can drastically reduce office space needs.

5. Implement Lean Practices

- o Lean practices focus on reducing waste and improving efficiency in all areas of business operations, from manufacturing to customer service.

- o By implementing a lean approach, startups can optimize their supply chain, minimize inventory costs, and eliminate non-essential spending.

6.1.2 Employee and Labor Cost Management

1. Flexible Work Arrangements

   o   Offer flexible work arrangements or remote work options to reduce office space and utility costs.

   o   This can also help improve employee satisfaction and retention, reducing the need for frequent hiring and training.

2. Hire Freelancers or Contractors

   o   Instead of hiring full-time employees for every role, consider using freelancers or contractors for specific projects or tasks. This gives you access to high-quality talent without the overhead costs of permanent employment (e.g., benefits, insurance, training, etc.).

3. Employee Incentive Plans

   o   Instead of offering large salary increments, startups can opt for equity compensation or stock options to incentivize employees. This reduces immediate cash expenses while aligning the employees' interests with the success of the company.

4. Cross-Training Employees

   o   Cross-train employees in multiple areas of the business. This allows for more flexibility and reduces the need to hire additional staff as the company grows.

6.1.3 Marketing and Sales Cost Reduction

1.   Leverage Digital Marketing

   o   Social media marketing (Facebook, Instagram, LinkedIn, etc.) and content marketing (blogs, podcasts, videos) can be highly effective and low-cost methods to reach potential customers.

   o   Focus on search engine optimization (SEO) to improve organic search traffic and reduce the need for paid ads.

2.   Referral and Word-of-Mouth Programs

   o   Encourage satisfied customers to refer others by offering them discounts or rewards. Referral programs are a low-cost marketing tool that can drive new business.

3.   Data-Driven Marketing

   o   Use analytics tools to track the success of marketing campaigns, identify profitable channels, and eliminate underperforming strategies. By focusing on high-ROI marketing methods, startups can reduce their marketing spend while maximizing results.

6.1.4 Technology and Infrastructure Savings

1.   Cloud Computing

- o Cloud-based solutions allow startups to avoid heavy upfront costs related to purchasing and maintaining physical infrastructure.

  - o Software-as-a-service (SaaS) tools, such as Salesforce, Dropbox, and Amazon Web Services, offer affordable subscription models that provide access to enterprise-grade technology without capital expenditure.

2. Energy Efficiency

  - o Implement energy-efficient practices in the workplace (e.g., LED lighting, energy-efficient computers, and appliances) to reduce electricity bills.

  - o If your office is large, consider switching to renewable energy sources like solar power or negotiate with your utility provider for better rates.

6.2 Tax-saving tips and strategies for startups

Tax planning is essential for startups to reduce liabilities and increase profitability while ensuring compliance with tax laws. The Indian tax system allows several deductions and exemptions that can help startups save money.

Below are effective tax planning strategies for startups to reduce the amount of tax they owe while complying with the law.

6.2.1 Take Advantage of Tax Holidays and Exemptions under the Startup India Scheme

1. Section 80-IAC Tax Deduction

Under Section 80-IAC of the Income Tax Act, eligible startups that are certified by the Department for Promotion of Industry and Internal Trade (DPIIT) are allowed to claim 100% tax exemption on profits for a period of any three consecutive years out of the first 10 years from the date of incorporation.

Eligibility:

1. Type of Business

- Must be a Private Limited Company or LLP.

- The entity must be registered on or after 1st Apr 2016 but on or before 31st March 2030. (Amended by Finance Act 2025)

- The turnover of the startup should not exceed ₹100 crores in any financial year.

- The startup should not be formed by splitting or reconstructing an existing business.

- The startup must utilize new Plant & Machinery, not transferred from existing business.

2. Nature of Business

The start-up should be engaged in

- Innovation

- Development or improvement of products, processes, or services, or

- A scalable business model with a high potential for employment generation or wealth creation.

2. Tax Exemption on Capital Gains

The capital gains tax exemption is available for investments in eligible startups. This exemption helps investors receive tax relief when investing in startups.

3. Tax Exemption for Investments

Investments in startups through the **Fund of Funds for Startups (FFS)**, managed by SIDBI, are eligible for tax exemptions.

4. Section 56(2)(viib)

It exempts angel investors from paying tax on funds raised by startups under certain conditions.

5. Simplified Compliance

Startups benefit from simplified compliance under the **Startup India Action Plan**, including self-certification for labor and environmental laws.

6.2.2 Maximize Deductions and Credits

1. Research and Development (R&D) Deductions

Startups in the technology, pharmaceutical, and manufacturing sectors can claim significant deductions for research and development (R&D) activities under **Section 35** of the Income Tax Act. This deduction applies to companies that are actively engaged in innovation, design, or improving their products/services.

- Expenses Eligible for Deductions:

    o Cost of materials used in research.

    o Salaries of employees working on R&D.

    o Cost of patents and trademarks associated with research.

- Benefits Available:

    o Startups involved in R&D can claim a 100% deduction under Section 35(2AB) for any in-house R&D activities.

    o An additional benefit may be available for capital expenditure incurred on R&D, allowing startups to deduct these expenses.

The Indian government encourages innovation by offering tax benefits to companies willing to invest in research and development. Startups should ensure that they document R&D expenses meticulously to take full advantage of this benefit.

2. **Interest on Loans**

   o   Interest paid on business loans can be claimed as a tax deduction. If your startup has borrowed funds for working capital or equipment purchases, ensure to claim the interest deduction.

3. **Section 80G**: While Section 80G is primarily targeted at individuals, startups (as businesses) can also benefit from it, as follows:

(i) Deductions for Donations Made by Startups:

   • Startups that make donations to eligible charitable organizations or causes can claim a tax deduction under Section 80G.

   • Donations to charitable trusts, NGOs, universities, or research institutions can reduce the taxable income of the startup, resulting in lower taxes.

(ii) Corporate Social Responsibility (CSR):

   • Startups that engage in Corporate Social Responsibility (CSR) activities, such as donating funds to charities, educational institutions, or health-related causes, can claim deductions under Section 80G.

   • Section 80G benefits are available for donations made in cash or in kind. However, the donation must be made to an eligible charity or institution that is recognized by the Income Tax Department.

4. Section 10AA: SEZ (Special Economic Zone) Benefits

Startups set up in Special Economic Zones (SEZs) and involved in manufacturing or providing services (including software, IT, and other services) can benefit from tax exemptions under Section 10AA of the Income Tax Act.

This allows a 100% tax exemption on profits earned from a Special Economic Zone (SEZ) for the first five years.

After the initial 5-year period, the exemption gradually reduces:

- 50% of the profits for the next 5 years.

- 50% of the profits can be claimed for another 5 years, but the exemption is subject to certain conditions (e.g., reinvestment of profits into the business).

- And partial exemption in subsequent years based on certain conditions.

5. Section 80-IB(10) – Deduction for Profits from Housing Projects

Startups involved in real estate development or housing projects can claim deductions under Section 80-IB(10), subject to certain conditions.

- Eligibility:

- o The property should be an affordable residential housing project.

- o The project should meet certain size and timeline criteria.

- o The deduction applies to profits from the development and sale of residential houses.

- Tax Benefit:

- o A 100% deduction of profits can be claimed for a qualifying housing project under this section for 5 years from the date of completion of the project.

6. Section 10A – Deduction for 100% Export Oriented Unit (EOU)

Section 10A provides a 100% tax exemption on the profits of an export-oriented unit (EOU) that is set up in Special Economic Zones (SEZs) or Software Technology Park (STP) for businesses involved in Software Technology or IT-enabled services.

This section is highly beneficial for tech startups and IT companies that focus on the export of services.

- Eligibility:

- o The company must be located in a Special Economic Zone.

- o The company must be engaged in the export of goods or services.

- Tax Benefit:

  o   Provides a 100% tax deduction on the profits of an eligible startup for the first 5 years of operations.

  o   After that, 50% for the next 5 years.

7. Section 80JJAA – Deduction for Employment of New Employees (Employer Benefits)

Section 80JJAA offers a significant tax deduction to employers who hire new employees, thereby incentivizing employment generation in the country. The key benefits for employers include:

- 30% deduction of the wages paid to new employees.

- Applicable for 3 years for each employee.

- Helps reduce the cost of hiring and retaining employees, especially for SMEs and businesses looking to scale.

- Aims to boost employment and create more job opportunities.

For businesses, Section 80JJAA can be a valuable tool for managing tax liabilities while contributing to the country's employment growth.

However, employers must ensure they meet all the criteria, such as employee eligibility, employment duration, and other documentation requirements, to claim this deduction.

6.2.3 Maximizing Depreciation Benefits - Investment in Plant and Machinery by Startups

Depreciation plays a vital role in tax planning for any business. It allows you to reduce taxable profits by accounting for the wear and tear of your business assets. Depreciation can be calculated on both tangible and intangible assets, and the rate of depreciation depends on the asset's useful life.

Under Section 32, businesses are eligible for depreciation on assets like plant and machinery, office equipment, and even vehicles. The rates vary based on the type of assets, but startups should ensure that they claim depreciation on all qualifying assets.

Depreciation is an essential tool for reducing taxable income and can save substantial taxes.

Additional Depreciation:

A taxpayer may claim additional depreciation (usually at 20%) on new plant and machinery (excluding buildings, furniture, and fittings) if the machinery is acquired and used in the same financial year.

How Depreciation Works:

For example, let's say a startup purchases a new computer for ₹50,000. Over 5 years, the depreciation for the computer would reduce the company's taxable income each year. The benefit is that the startup pays fewer taxes during this period, which can help conserve cash flow in the early stages of business.

6.3 Other Tax Planning Strategies for Startups

Effective tax planning is not just about reducing the amount of tax paid but also about planning ahead to avoid future liabilities. Here are some effective tax planning strategies for startups:

1. Choose the Right Business Structure

As we discussed in Chapter 3, the choice between a **Private Limited Company**, **LLP**, or **Sole Proprietorship** can have a significant impact on your tax obligations. While a Private Limited Company might have more compliance, it offers better tax benefits like lower corporate tax rates compared to Sole Proprietorships or Partnerships.

2. Invest in Capital Assets

Investing in capital assets, like machinery or equipment, helps your business save taxes through depreciation. Ensure that you optimize your capital expenditures to maximize depreciation benefits.

3. Income Splitting

For family-owned businesses, income splitting between family members can be a useful strategy. Income splitting helps to reduce the overall tax burden by distributing income across lower tax brackets, provided all the family members are legally employed and the income is reasonable.

4. Keep Track of All Expenses

Every business incurs several expenses in day-to-day operations. From marketing expenses to office supplies, maintaining a clear record of these expenses allows you to deduct them from your taxable income. An organized system for tracking expenses is critical to ensure you're taking full advantage of allowable deductions.

6.4 Proper Tax Compliance to Avoid Penalties

1. Timely Filing of Returns

    o   Ensure that income tax returns, GST returns, and other statutory filings are submitted on time. Late submissions attract penalties and interest charges.

2. Maintain Accurate Books of Accounts

    o   Keep detailed and organized financial records. If your startup is subject to a tax audit, accurate records will help ensure compliance and reduce the risk of penalties.

3. Avoid Underreporting Income

    o   Always report your income accurately. Underreporting or hiding income to reduce tax liabilities can lead to severe penalties, including tax evasion charges.

CHAPTER 7

FINANCING YOUR STARTUP: FUNDS-RAISING AND FINANCIAL STRUCTURING

Securing the right financing is one of the most critical steps in building a successful startup. The funds you raise will help you scale your operations, invest in technology, hire talent, and market your products.

In this chapter, we will cover the different financing options available to startups, the process of raising funds, and how to strategically plan your funding rounds.

We will also delve into the pros and cons of each financing method and offer advice on how to choose the best option for your business.

When your startup needs funding, it's essential to understand the tax and compliance implications of different funding sources.

7.1 Understanding Your Financial Needs

Before you begin exploring financing options, it's essential to clearly understand your financial needs. This will help you determine how much capital you need to raise, what milestones you aim to achieve, and what type of investment would suit your business at various stages.

Key Questions to Ask Before Seeking Funds:

1. **How much capital do you need?**

   o   Consider your operating expenses, salaries, marketing costs, and the investment required for product development or expansion.

   o   Financial forecasts and projections will help you calculate how much capital is required for the next 12-18 months.

2. **What stage is your startup at?**

   o   Seed stage (concept or early prototype).

   o   Growth stage (early revenue, customer base, and product-market fit).

   o   Scaling stage (expansion, large market, increasing revenues).

3. **How will you utilize the funds?**

   o   Whether it's for marketing, hiring key talent, or technology infrastructure, investors will want to know how their money will be used.

4. **How much equity are you willing to give up?**

   o   Different types of funding come with varying levels of equity or debt obligations.

Develop a Financial Model and Budget:

- Develop a detailed **financial model** that includes revenue projections, expense forecasts, and profit margins.

- Prepare a **budget** outlining how the funds will be spent and how much runway you expect (how long the funds will sustain your business).

7.2 Fund Raising & Equity Financing

7.2.1 Bootstrapping: Self-Funding Your Startup

Bootstrapping refers to funding your startup from your personal savings or revenue generated by the business.

While this approach gives you full control over your business, it can be risky if your personal finances are tied to the venture's success.

Advantages of Bootstrapping:

1. Full Control: You retain full ownership of the business without having to answer to external investors.

2. No Debt: You avoid the pressures of loan repayment or giving up equity in the business.

3. Faster Decision-Making: With no external investors, you can make decisions quickly and execute your vision without needing approval.

Disadvantages of Bootstrapping:

1. Limited Resources: Self-funding may not be enough to cover all your startup's needs, especially in the early stages.

2. Personal Risk: If the business fails, you risk losing your personal savings.

3. Slow Growth: Without external capital, your ability to scale may be limited, especially if you're relying on slow and steady revenue growth.

When Should You Bootstrap?

- Bootstrapping is ideal in the early stages when your business requires limited capital or when you have a clear pathway to profitability.

- It's also appropriate when you have personal savings that you are willing to invest and you are confident in your ability to generate cash flow quickly.

7.2.2 Raising Funds from Friends and Family

Many entrepreneurs start by raising funds from friends and family, especially when they are at an early stage and have limited access to formal sources of capital.

Advantages of Raising Funds from Friends and Family:

1. Quick Access: It can be faster to raise money from friends and family than going through formal investment routes.

2. Flexible Terms: You may have more flexibility in terms of repayment, equity, and control compared to institutional investors.

3. Less Formality: There is less bureaucracy and paperwork compared to venture capital or angel investment.

Risks and Disadvantages:

1. Personal Relationships: Mixing business with personal relationships can be risky. If the business fails, it can damage personal relationships.

2. Lack of Expertise: Family and friends may not bring any strategic guidance or expertise to the business.

3. Limited Amount of Capital: The funds raised from friends and family may not be enough to fuel long-term growth.

Tips for Raising Funds from Friends and Family:

1. Clearly Define the Terms: Create a formal loan or equity agreement to prevent misunderstandings later.

2. Prepare for the Worst: Be transparent about the risks involved in the business, and make sure your friends and family understand that there is no guarantee of success.

3. Put It in Writing: Always document the terms, investment amount, and repayment schedule. This avoids conflicts down the road.

7.2.3 Angel Investors: Early-Stage Funding

Angel investors are individuals who provide capital to startups in exchange for equity or debt. Angel investors often come in during the seed stage, providing the financial push needed to take a product to market or develop the business further.

Advantages of Angel Investors:

1. Flexible Terms: Angel investors often offer more favorable terms compared to venture capital firms.

2. Mentorship and Networking: Angels typically bring experience, mentorship, and industry connections to the table, which can help accelerate business growth.

3. Relatively Quick Funding: Angels tend to make decisions faster than venture capital firms, allowing startups to raise funds quickly.

Disadvantages of Angel Investors:

1. Loss of Equity: In exchange for funding, angel investors typically ask for a share of equity, which means giving up some level of control.

2. Lack of Professionalism: Not all angel investors have the expertise or commitment to help your business grow.

3. Investor Expectations: Angels often expect a fast return on their investment, putting pressure on the business to scale quickly.

How to Attract Angel Investors:

1. Develop a Strong Business Plan: Prepare a clear, concise, and compelling business plan that outlines your vision, market opportunity, and financial projections.

2. Show Traction: Investors want to see evidence of product-market fit or early traction, like user adoption, revenue, or significant partnerships.

3. Network: Attend startup events, pitch competitions, and angel investor networks to meet potential investors.

7.2.4 Venture Capital (VC): Funding for Growth and Expansion

Venture capital is a common source of funding for startups that are already past the seed stage and need significant capital to scale. VC firms invest larger amounts of money in exchange for equity and usually have high expectations for returns.

Advantages of Venture Capital:

1. Large Funding Amounts: VCs provide significant capital that can be used to scale operations, expand into new markets, or develop new products.

2. Expertise and Guidance: Venture capitalists typically bring a wealth of experience and strategic guidance, often sitting on your startup's board and providing valuable insights.

3. Networking: VCs often introduce startups to other businesses, partners, or potential customers, leveraging their networks to benefit your startup.

Disadvantages of Venture Capital:

1. Loss of Control: VCs typically want significant ownership and control in the company, which may dilute the founders' stake and decision-making power.

2. High Expectations for Growth: Venture capitalists expect rapid scaling and a clear exit strategy, such as an IPO or acquisition, within a few years.

3. Pressure to Perform: With the influx of capital, there is considerable pressure to perform and deliver returns, which can lead to stress and challenging decision-making.

How to Approach Venture Capitalists:

1. Prepare for Rigorous Due Diligence: VCs will conduct extensive due diligence, reviewing your business model, financials, team, and market opportunity. Be prepared with all relevant documents.

2. Understand Their Expectations: VCs expect high growth and quick returns. Be ready to align your business strategy with their goals.

3. Pitch Perfectly: Your pitch to VCs must be compelling, concise, and backed by solid data that demonstrates the potential for significant returns.

7.2.5 Government Funding and Grants in India

The Indian government offers several programs and initiatives aimed at promoting entrepreneurship and helping startups get off the ground.

These initiatives provide access to low-interest loans, grants, and subsidies.

Key Government Schemes:

1. Startup India Scheme: This initiative provides several benefits to startups, including tax exemptions, access to government funding, and easier regulatory processes.

2. MUDRA Loan Scheme: Under this scheme, micro-enterprises can receive loans without collateral, which can be a helpful funding option for early-stage startups.

3. SIDBI Scheme: The Small Industries Development Bank of India (SIDBI) offers a variety of schemes for MSMEs (Micro, Small, and Medium Enterprises) to access financial support.

How to Leverage Government Funding:

1. Understand Eligibility: Government schemes have specific eligibility criteria. Research the schemes to determine which one fits your startup.

2. Prepare Required Documentation: Ensure that you have the necessary documents, such as a business plan, financial statements, and tax returns, to apply for government funding.

3. Consult Professionals: Work with financial experts or consultants to help navigate the complexities of government funding processes.

7.2.6 Crowdfunding: Raising Small Amounts from a Large Pool

Crowdfunding has emerged as a viable alternative for raising funds by collecting small contributions from a large group of people, often via online platforms like Kickstarter, Indiegogo, or Ketto.

Advantages of Crowdfunding:

1. Access to Capital: Crowdfunding allows you to raise funds without giving up equity or incurring debt.

2. Market Validation: Successfully raising funds through crowdfunding can validate your idea and demonstrate demand to investors.

3. Marketing Opportunity: Crowdfunding platforms can also serve as marketing tools, giving your product visibility to a large audience.

Disadvantages of Crowdfunding:

1. Time-Consuming: Running a crowdfunding campaign requires substantial marketing effort and preparation to attract backers.

2. Risk of Failure: Not every crowdfunding campaign meets its funding goals. If you fail to reach your target, you might not receive any funds.

3. Intellectual Property Risks: Publicly sharing your ideas or prototypes on crowdfunding platforms might expose your business to the risk of imitation.

Best Practices for Crowdfunding Success:

1. Develop a Compelling Story: Your campaign should tell a compelling story and highlight why your product is valuable and unique.

2. Offer Attractive Rewards: Provide enticing rewards or incentives for backers to motivate them to contribute.

3. Engage Early: Build a community before launching your crowdfunding campaign to ensure you have an initial base of supporters.

7.3 Debt Financing

Debt financing involves borrowing money from banks or financial institutions that must be repaid with interest. While debt financing can be quicker to access than equity financing, it also comes with the obligation to repay the principal and interest, which can be burdensome for a cash-strapped startup.

Types of Debt Financing:

7.3.1 Term Loans

Term loans are one of the most traditional forms of debt financing. In this arrangement, a startup borrows a lump sum amount from a bank or financial institution and repays it over a fixed period with interest. These loans are typically used for long-term investments, such as purchasing equipment, expanding operations, or infrastructure.

Features:

- Fixed loan amount with regular repayments.

- Interest rates can be fixed or variable.

- Suitable for specific investments, such as buying machinery or setting up new business facilities.

Available From:

- Banks (e.g., State Bank of India, HDFC Bank, ICICI Bank)

- Non-Banking Financial Companies (NBFCs) like Bajaj Finserv,
  L&T Finance, etc.

7.3.2 Working Capital Loans

Working capital loans are designed to cover a startup's day-to-day operational expenses, such as paying for raw materials, salaries, utilities, or short-term expenses. These loans provide the flexibility to borrow a certain amount and repay it as the business generates cash flow.

Features:

- Short-term financing for everyday operations.

- It can be either secured (against assets) or unsecured.

- Repayments are generally linked to the cash flow cycle.

Available From: Banks and NBFCs.

7.3.3 Government Schemes & Grants

The Government of India offers various schemes, grants, and incentives to support startups, especially in their initial stages. These schemes are designed to make financing more accessible to entrepreneurs.

Key Government Schemes:

- **Pradhan Mantri Mudra Yojana (PMMY):** Offers small loans (up to ₹10 lakhs) for non-corporate, non-farm small/micro enterprises.

The loan is available in three categories: Shishu (up to ₹50,000), Kishore (₹50,000 to ₹5 lakhs), and Tarun (₹5 lakhs to ₹10 lakhs).

Available From: Public sector banks, NBFCs, and Microfinance institutions (MFIs) online on the Udyami Mitra portal.

- **Stand-Up India Scheme**: Provides loans to SC / ST/women entrepreneurs to promote **greenfield enterprises (first-time venture of the beneficiary)**. The loan is available up to ₹10 lakh, which was recently extended to ₹1 crore.

Up to 18 months moratorium period – pay only interest amount.

Up to 85% project funding.

Applicant must be 18+ with no previous loan default

Features:

- Easy accessibility for micro and small businesses.

- No Collateral is required.

- Lower interest rates.

- Subsidized loans and grants.

- Less stringent eligibility requirements and lower collateral.

Available From: Online on standupmitra.in

7.3.4 Invoice Financing (Factoring)

Invoice financing, or factoring, involves selling unpaid invoices to a third party (a factor) at a discount. The factor immediately provides the startup with cash, typically around 80-90% of the invoice value, and collects the payment from the customers.

Features:

- Quick access to capital by using outstanding invoices as collateral.

- It can be more expensive than traditional loans due to higher interest rates.

- Ideal for startups that have a large number of invoices pending payment.

Available From: Fintech lenders and specialized companies such as KredX, Finbox, and others.

7.3.5 Line of Credit

A flexible financing option where you can borrow money up to a certain limit as and when needed.

A Line of Credit is a revolving credit facility extended by a bank or financial institution, allowing a business to borrow funds up to an approved limit. It is designed to provide flexible, short-term financing for any operational need.

Features:

- Flexible borrowing and repayment.

- Interest is only charged on the amount drawn.

- Commonly used for inventory purchases or bridging cash flow gaps.

Available From: Banks (e.g., HDFC, Axis Bank, ICICI).

7.3.6 CGTMSE (Credit Guarantee Fund Trust for Micro and Small Enterprises) Loans

CGTMSE is a scheme launched by the Government of India in collaboration with the Ministry of MSME and SIDBI. The objective of this scheme is to provide guarantee cover for loans granted to micro and small enterprises (MSEs) by financial institutions without the need for collateral or third-party guarantees.

The scheme aims to encourage lending to micro and small businesses that otherwise may find it difficult to get loans due to lack of collateral or financial stability.

It helps these businesses access financing for growth, expansion, or other operational needs.

Eligibility:

- New & Existing MSMEs both. Must be MSME registered with the udhyam portal.

Features:

- The loan is available up to ₹5 crore (increased to ₹10 cr in Budget 2025)

- Collateral free, for both working capital and term loan

- Backed by Govt of India

- Easy accessibility for micro, small & medium businesses.

- Interest Subsidy – 1 % to 2 %

Available From: Banks and NBFCs.

7.3.7 PMEGP (Prime Minister's Employment Generation Programme) Loans

The PMEGP is a credit-linked subsidy scheme launched by the Government of India to generate employment opportunities in the country.

The PMEGP is primarily aimed at promoting **self-employment** and **entrepreneurship** among the youth, particularly in **rural and semi-urban areas**, by providing financial support for setting up micro-enterprises and small businesses.

Eligibility:

- Minimum age required: 18+.

- Minimum education required 8th standard.

- Available on new projects only

Features:

- Offer concessional interest rate + 15 % to 35% subsidy

- Subsidy to General - 15 % to 25%, and to SC/ST/Women - 25 % to 35%

- The loan is available up to ₹50 lakhs for manufacturers and ₹20 lakhs for service providers & trading

- 3 years bank FD lockin – implementing agency (e.g., KVIC/ KVIB/ DIC) forward a subsidy release letter after 3 years of satisfied usage of funds.

Available From: Apply Online at Jansamarth and get Loan disbursement from bank

8.3 Financial Structuring for Growth

A well-thought-out financial structure is crucial for the long-term success of any startup. Financial structuring involves how you manage your company's capital, which includes equity financing, debt financing, and internal funds.

The key to success in financial structuring is to balance risk and return while ensuring the company can meet its financial obligations.

Optimizing Capital Structure:

- Maintain a Balanced Debt-Equity Ratio: A balanced debt-to-equity ratio is essential for maintaining financial health. Too much debt can put unnecessary strain on cash flow, while too little equity may hinder growth potential.

- Monitor Cash Flow: Cash flow is the lifeblood of any business. Ensure you have adequate working capital to cover operational expenses and avoid cash crunches.

- Use Convertible Debts: Convertible debt allows the company to raise funds in the short term, with the option for the debt to convert into equity at a later date. This is a great option for startups looking to avoid immediate dilution of ownership.

7.4 Exit Strategy and Valuation

As you raise capital and grow your startup, having a clear exit strategy is essential. Exit strategies define how investors and founders will exit the business while making a profit. Common exit strategies include:

- Initial Public Offering (IPO): Going public by issuing shares on the stock exchange.

- Acquisition: Selling the business to a larger company or strategic partner.

- Mergers: Merging with another business to form a more prominent entity.

Valuation of Startups:

Valuing a startup can be challenging, as many are pre-revenue or have minimal assets. However, valuation plays a significant role in securing funding and determining equity ownership. Common methods to value a startup include the Discounted Cash Flow (DCF) Method, Market Comparison, and the Risk Factor Summation method.

CHAPTER 8

Legal Challenges and How to Avoid Common Pitfalls

Legal issues are a significant concern for startups. While many entrepreneurs are focused on growing their businesses, understanding and addressing legal matters early on can save a lot of trouble in the future. Startups that are built on a solid legal foundation tend to be more resilient to challenges and risks. In this chapter, we will discuss common legal challenges startups face, key legal requirements, and how to avoid the most common legal pitfalls.

8.1 Business Ideas and Intellectual Property Protection

Intellectual property refers to creations of the mind, such as inventions, designs, trademarks, and literary and artistic works. IP allows the owner to have exclusive rights to their creations.

Key Types of Intellectual Property:

1. **Patents**: Patents protect new inventions, processes, or technological advancements. Patents grant exclusive rights to the inventor for a set period (usually 20 years).

- **Importance**: For startups developing new technology, products, or processes, a patent can prevent others from copying or using the invention without permission.

- **Filing Process**: In India, startups can file patents with the **Indian Patent Office**. It is advisable to work with patent lawyers or IP specialists to ensure that the patent is drafted properly.

2. **Trademarks**: A trademark protects symbols, logos, names, and other identifiers that distinguish your products or services.

    - **Importance**: A strong brand identity is crucial for startups, and a trademark protects that identity from being imitated. This is especially vital when entering competitive markets.

    - **Filing Process**: Trademarks can be registered with the **Trade Marks Registry** under the **Office of the Controller General of Patents, Designs, and Trade Marks**. Registration grants exclusive rights to use the trademark in India.

3. **Copyrights**: Copyright protects original works of authorship, such as software, music, artwork, and written works.

    - **Importance**: If your startup creates original content—whether software code, written blogs, or even branding materials—copyrights ensure that others cannot reproduce or profit from your work without permission.

4. **Trade Secrets**: A trade secret refers to any information (business processes, formulas, techniques) that is confidential and provides a competitive advantage.

   o **Importance**: Startups need to protect sensitive business information (e.g., algorithms, customer lists, or business strategies) that is not publicly disclosed but is critical to business success.

   o **Protection**: Ensure employees and contractors sign **Non-Disclosure Agreements (NDAs)** and **Non-Compete Agreements (NCAs)** to safeguard your trade secrets.

Steps to Protect Your IP:

- **Legal Registration**: Ensure all patents, trademarks, and copyrights are registered with the relevant authorities. This provides a legal foundation to protect and enforce your IP rights.

- **Document Everything**: Keep thorough records of your IP creations, including design drafts, ideas, and conversations with potential partners. This will be crucial if you need to prove ownership.

- **Use NDAs and Legal Contracts**: When working with third parties (contractors, investors, employees), ensure they sign NDAs to prevent the unauthorized sharing of your confidential information.

8.2 Contract Management

Contracts are the legal backbone of business relationships, and managing them properly is essential to avoid disputes and potential lawsuits. Contracts outline the terms and conditions of agreements, expectations, and the legal obligations of all parties involved.

Types of Key Contracts for Startups:

1. **Founders' Agreement:**

    o   **Purpose**: The founders' agreement is essential in establishing the roles, responsibilities, and expectations of each co-founder. This agreement addresses equity splits, decision-making processes, dispute resolution, and the exit strategy of co-founders.

    o   **Importance**: It prevents future conflicts and misunderstandings by clearly defining the terms of the business's management and the equity stakes of each founder.

2. **Employment Contracts:**

    o   **Purpose**: Employment contracts outline the relationship between the employer (your startup) and the employee. These contracts should define job responsibilities, compensation, non-disclosure clauses, non-compete clauses, and grounds for termination.

- o **Importance**: Proper employment contracts ensure that employees are clear on their roles and responsibilities and can prevent disputes regarding severance, compensation, or other employment terms.

3. **Non-Disclosure Agreements (NDAs)**:

   - o **Purpose**: NDAs are used to protect confidential information shared between parties. This is especially important when discussing sensitive matters like product plans, trade secrets, and business strategies.

   - o **Importance**: NDAs legally bind parties to keep information confidential, thus reducing the risk of leaks or theft of proprietary information.

   - o **When to Use**: NDAs should be used when hiring employees, engaging with potential investors, working with suppliers, or entering partnerships.

4. **Service and Supplier Contracts**:

   - o **Purpose**: These contracts govern the terms of the relationship between your startup and external suppliers or service providers. They should include details like payment terms, delivery timelines, and the scope of services.

   - o **Importance**: Ensuring that these contracts are clear and legally binding helps avoid disputes over delays, quality issues, or payment terms.

5. **Investment Agreements**:

- o **Purpose**: If your startup raises capital from investors, an investment agreement outlines the terms of the investment, including equity stakes, rights, obligations, and the exit strategy.

- o **Importance**: These agreements set clear expectations with investors and protect the founders and the business.

Best Practices for Contract Management:

- **Legal Review**: Have all contracts reviewed by qualified professionals to ensure they are legally sound and enforceable.

- **Clarity**: Ensure that all contracts are clear and unambiguous and cover all potential scenarios (e.g., what happens if the business is sold or an employee leaves).

- **Record Keeping**: Keep copies of all signed agreements in a secure, organized manner. Digital solutions like cloud storage can help ensure that contracts are easily accessible and safe.

8.3 Dispute Management and Resolution

Disputes are inevitable in any business, especially as startups interact with various parties like customers, suppliers, partners, and investors. The key is to manage disputes effectively and resolve them quickly to avoid long-term damage to the business.

Common Startup Disputes:

1. **Intellectual Property Disputes**: IP theft or infringement is one of the most common types of disputes startups face, particularly when their ideas are copied or misused.

2. **Founder Disputes**: Differences in vision, work ethic, or equity distribution among co-founders can lead to disputes that disrupt business operations.

3. **Customer or Supplier Disputes**: Disagreements over service quality, payment terms, or contract fulfillment can result in legal action.

4. **Employment Disputes**: Conflicts over salaries, termination, or harassment can lead to legal action by employees.

Dispute Resolution Mechanisms:

1. **Negotiation**: Direct discussions between the parties involved to resolve the dispute amicably.

   o **Advantages**: Fast, informal, and cost-effective. It can preserve business relationships.

   o **When to Use**: When both parties are open to compromise and seek an out-of-court resolution.

2. **Mediation**: A neutral third party (mediator) helps the parties reach a mutually acceptable solution.

o **Advantages**: Less formal than litigation, quicker, and generally more cost-effective. Mediators help facilitate communication between parties.

o **When to Use**: When negotiation fails, both parties still want to resolve the issue outside of court.

3. **Arbitration**: A more formal method of dispute resolution where an arbitrator listens to both sides and makes a binding decision.

o **Advantages**: Faster and cheaper than litigation. The decision is legally binding and can be enforced in court.

o **When to Use**: When both parties agree to binding arbitration and want a quicker, definitive resolution than what court trials provide.

4. **Litigation**: Taking legal action in a court of law to resolve a dispute.

o **Advantages**: The decision is legally binding and enforceable. It provides a final resolution.

o **When to Use**: When the dispute cannot be resolved through other means or when one party refuses to negotiate or arbitrate.

Preventing Disputes:

- **Clear Agreements**: Ensure that all contracts and agreements are well-defined and detailed to prevent misunderstandings.

- **Regular Communication**: Keep open lines of communication with all stakeholders (employees, partners, suppliers, etc.) to resolve issues before they escalate into disputes.

- **Legal Counsel**: Having a good relationship with a lawyer or legal advisor can help prevent disputes by offering proactive advice on potential legal pitfalls.

Conclusion

Navigating legal challenges is a crucial aspect of running a startup, and addressing them early on can save time, money, and reputation in the

long run. By focusing on protecting intellectual property, creating solid contracts, and having dispute resolution mechanisms in place, startups can build a strong legal foundation that supports their growth and shields them from common pitfalls. Legal considerations may seem overwhelming at first, but by taking proactive steps and seeking expert advice, founders can mitigate risks and focus on building a sustainable business.

CHAPTER 9

SCALING UP: TRANSITIONING FROM A STARTUP TO A GROWING BUSINESS

Scaling a business is one of the most challenging phases in the lifecycle of a startup. It involves moving from a small, nimble operation to a larger, more complex organization. Scaling a business requires more than just increasing sales.

As your startup grows, it becomes increasingly important to refine operational strategies, improve financial management, and streamline regulatory compliance. Transitioning into a larger business requires planning for scaling, market expansion, and higher regulatory scrutiny.

The goal of scaling is to increase revenue without a corresponding increase in costs. This chapter will explore the strategies, processes, and key considerations for startups as they transition to established businesses.

9.1 Understanding the Need for Scaling Up

Scaling is not merely about growth in revenue or customer base; it's about ensuring that your business is structured to handle increased demands efficiently. This involves:

- **Operational Efficiencies**: Streamlining internal processes to manage higher volumes without a linear increase in costs.

- **Market Expansion**: Growing your customer base, possibly by entering new geographic markets or diversifying your product offerings.

- **Financial Health**: Scaling requires investment in infrastructure, human resources, and technology, which can strain cash flows if not planned carefully.

Signs That Your Startup Is Ready to Scale:

1. **Stable Revenue**: When you have a consistent revenue stream and predictable cash flow, you can confidently plan for scaling.

2. **Market Demand**: If your products or services are in demand and you're seeing consistent sales growth, it's time to explore scaling.

3. **Operational Systems in Place**: When you have robust systems for managing operations (inventory, customer service, etc.), it becomes easier to expand without compromising quality.

9.2 Operational Scaling: Streamlining Processes

Efficient operational management is the backbone of scaling. It involves fine-tuning processes and ensuring that as demand increases, your operations can handle the load. Let's look at the critical areas of operational scaling.

1. Automating Processes:

As you scale, relying on manual processes can become inefficient and prone to errors. **Automation** helps you handle repetitive tasks quickly and with minimal human input. For example:

- **Accounting and Financial Management**: Use accounting software like **QuickBooks** or **Tally** to automate invoicing, expense tracking, and tax calculations.

- **Inventory Management**: Systems like **Zoho Inventory** or **TradeGecko** can automate stock tracking, order processing, and even restocking.

2. Supply Chain Management:

With scaling, your supply chain will become more complex. It's essential to establish relationships with suppliers who can handle larger orders and provide better terms. For example, consider:

- **Supplier Negotiations**: Negotiate long-term contracts with suppliers for better pricing and payment terms as you scale.

- **Logistics**: Work with logistics partners who can scale with you, whether it's local courier services or global shipping providers. Consider third-party logistics (3PL) companies for managing warehousing, fulfillment, and shipping.

3. Data-Driven Decision Making:

As your startup grows, the volume of data increases. Utilize tools like **Google Analytics**, **CRM systems**, or **ERP software** to track key performance metrics (KPIs) and customer data. Data will help guide decisions in marketing, product development, and even customer service.

4. Standardizing Operations:

Startups often operate with flexible or ad-hoc processes. However, scaling requires creating standardized systems across departments like marketing, HR, and operations. For example:

- **Marketing**: Develop a clear content marketing strategy, utilize automated email marketing campaigns, and have a consistent customer acquisition strategy.

- **HR**: Create standardized processes for onboarding, training, and employee evaluation to ensure consistency as the team grows.

9.3 Financial Considerations for Scaling

Scaling requires a significant investment in both human and financial resources. A well-managed financial strategy is crucial to ensure that you have the necessary capital to fund growth without overextending.

1. Funding Your Expansion:

At this stage, startups need access to funding to scale operations. Here are some common ways to raise funds:

- **Equity Financing**: If you haven't already done so, consider raising funds from venture capital (VC) or angel investors. As your company grows, investors will want to see a clear plan for scaling and increased profitability.

- **Debt Financing**: If you don't want to dilute equity, debt financing from banks or financial institutions can be an option. However, you must ensure your cash flow can support the repayment.

- **Government Schemes**: Various government schemes like **MUDRA Loans, Startup India**, and **SIDBI funding** offer financing options with lower interest rates for scaling businesses.

2. Managing Cash Flow:

When scaling, you might face significant upfront costs, such as:

- **Hiring Costs**: As you expand, you'll need to hire more employees, which increases payroll expenses.

- **Infrastructure Investment**: Whether it's purchasing new equipment, upgrading your technology, or expanding your office space, these are all capital-intensive expenditures.

Managing cash flow is critical during this phase. Implement strategies such as:

- **Establishing an Emergency Fund**: Having a financial cushion ensures that you don't run into liquidity issues during periods of rapid expansion.

- **Invoicing and Collection**: Set up automated invoicing systems and ensure prompt collection of payments to maintain a healthy cash flow.

3. Profitability vs. Growth:

During the scaling phase, startups often face a dilemma: Do they focus on profitability, or is it more important to focus on growth? Many startups prioritize growth at the expense of profitability (e.g., by reinvesting profits into expansion). While this can lead to faster scaling, it's essential to keep an eye on profitability metrics and ensure that the company doesn't grow too quickly without ensuring sustainable profits.

9.4 Talent Acquisition and Management

As you scale, your human resources strategy becomes even more important. To support growth, you'll need a strong team of talented individuals across various departments.

1. Hiring the Right People:

Your initial team may have been small and highly skilled, but as you grow, you'll need to hire specialized talent. When scaling, hire employees with skills that align with your growth strategy, whether it's marketing, product development, or operations.

- **Recruitment Process**: Invest in professional HR software like **BambooHR** or **Workable** to streamline your recruitment process.

- **Focus on Culture Fit**: As you hire, make sure that new employees align with your company's culture. A strong company culture is essential for long-term success, especially when you grow from a startup into an established business.

2. Leadership Development:

Effective leadership is crucial for managing a growing organization. As a founder, you may have been the driving force behind the initial success, but as you scale, delegating responsibilities becomes important.

Invest in leadership development programs for existing employees and hire senior managers with experience scaling businesses.

3. Retaining Talent:

High turnover can be costly during scaling. To retain employees, offer competitive compensation packages, professional growth opportunities, and a positive work environment.

Startups that offer **equity options** can also keep employees motivated by giving them a sense of ownership in the business.

9.5 Marketing and Customer Acquisition Strategies for Scaling

When scaling, customer acquisition becomes more complex. You need to adopt strategies that allow you to grow your customer base efficiently while maintaining brand consistency.

1. Expanding Your Target Market:

Initially, you may have been focusing on a niche market. As you scale, consider expanding your target market by introducing new products or services that appeal to a broader audience. You can also consider geographic expansion, either nationally or internationally.

2. Marketing Automation:

Marketing automation tools like **HubSpot**, **Mailchimp**, or **Marketo** allow you to manage large-scale marketing campaigns efficiently. Automating email campaigns, social media posts, and customer segmentation can help you reach a larger audience without a proportional increase in marketing costs.

3. Scaling Customer Support:

As your customer base grows, customer support becomes crucial. To scale customer service, consider:

- **Self-Service Options**: Develop comprehensive FAQs, video tutorials, and knowledge bases to help customers help themselves.

- **Chatbots and AI**: Implement AI-powered chatbots for 24/7 support.

- **Outsourcing Support**: If customer support volumes increase significantly, consider outsourcing customer service to specialized agencies to maintain high service standards.

4. Brand Awareness:

At this stage, brand awareness becomes critical. To build your brand presence, consider investing in:

- **Content Marketing**: Create high-quality, valuable content like blogs, case studies, and whitepapers to educate your audience and establish authority.

- **Influencer Partnerships**: Work with influencers in your industry to reach larger audiences.

- **Public Relations (PR)**: Hire a PR firm to handle media relations, press releases, and public outreach.

9.6 Technology Infrastructure and Scalability

As your business grows, so does the need for scalable technology solutions. Choosing the right technology infrastructure is essential to handle increased demand efficiently.

1. Cloud Solutions:

Investing in cloud-based software and infrastructure can save costs and scale with ease. Platforms like **AWS, Google Cloud**, or **Microsoft Azure** allow startups to scale up or down depending on demand without investing in physical hardware.

2. Data Security:

As your company grows, the volume of sensitive data increases. You must ensure that your IT systems are secure and that you comply with data protection regulations like the **GDPR** or **India's IT Act**.

3. Enterprise Resource Planning (ERP):

Implementing an **ERP system** helps streamline operations across various departments (finance, HR, sales, etc.). ERP systems like **SAP** or **Oracle NetSuite** are essential for managing multiple departments efficiently.

9.7 Tax Implications & Various Compliances: As your turnover crosses certain limits, you may face higher tax rates and more complex compliance procedures. Various Compliances increase with the increase in turnover, profits, capital, etc.

Tax Implications:

1. Change in Tax Structure:

    o   As the business scales, it may no longer qualify for certain startup tax exemptions (like those under Section 80-IAC or tax benefits related to MSME status). Transitioning to a larger business often means a shift to different tax categories, such as corporate tax rates or GST registrations for larger operations.

o   If the business expands internationally, it could face issues related to transfer pricing, cross-border taxation, and compliance with tax laws in foreign jurisdictions.

2. Increased Tax Compliance:

o   Larger businesses are subject to more detailed tax filings and documentation. This includes quarterly GST returns, TDS (Tax Deducted at Source) filings, and more complex income tax returns with greater scrutiny from tax authorities.

o   The company may need to deal with new compliance aspects, such as audit requirements, and ensure adherence to various tax laws applicable to larger businesses.

3. Capital Gains and Tax Planning:

o   Businesses that scale up often seek funding through equity financing or debt financing, which brings with it capital gains tax considerations on the sale of shares or assets. Careful planning around these taxes can help optimize returns.

o   Planning for long-term capital gains (LTCG) and short-term capital gains (STCG) taxes becomes important, especially if the company holds assets that appreciate over time.

Compliances:

1. Regulatory Filings and Licenses:

   o As the business grows, the compliance burden increases. It may need to apply for additional licenses and permits relevant to its new activities or larger scale of operations, such as environmental approvals, industry-specific licenses, or import-export regulations.

   o Regular filings with ROC (Registrar of Companies), SEBI (Securities and Exchange Board of India) (if applicable), and other regulatory bodies become more frequent and detailed.

2. Labor and Employment Laws:

   o Scaling up often involves hiring more employees. As the workforce expands, compliance with labor laws (such as EPF, ESI, and Gratuity contributions) becomes more important. Additionally, larger businesses must ensure compliance with the Minimum Wages Act, Industrial Disputes Act, and other employment-related regulations.

3. GST and Other Indirect Taxes:

   o Once the business exceeds the prescribed turnover limit, GST registration becomes mandatory. Additionally, compliance with GST returns, invoice requirements, and input tax credit claims needs to be handled efficiently to avoid penalties.

o   Other indirect taxes like customs duties and excise duties (for certain manufacturing businesses) will also become applicable.

4. Financial Reporting & Audits:

o   As the business grows, financial reporting must comply with Indian Accounting Standards (Ind-AS) or Accounting Standards (AS) for larger businesses. This includes preparing detailed annual financial statements, which will need to be audited.

o   Regular statutory audits and internal audits are required to maintain transparency and ensure that the company adheres to tax laws and corporate governance standards.

Conclusion

Scaling up is a transformative phase for any startup. It involves managing increasing complexity across operations, finances, and human resources. By focusing on automation, optimizing financial planning, expanding market reach, and investing in technology, startups can successfully transition from a small operation to a thriving business. The key to successful scaling is maintaining balance—ensuring that growth is sustainable, profitable, and aligned with the long-term vision of the company.

PRECAUTIONS TO BE TAKEN BY STARTUPS FOR COMPLIANCE AND TAXATION

While starting and running a business, entrepreneurs need to take several precautions to ensure they remain compliant with legal and tax regulations, avoid penalties, and maximize growth opportunities.

Taking these precautions early on can prevent costly mistakes later. Here are the key **precautions** that startup founders should take:

1. Choose the Right Business Structure

- **Precaution**: Don't rush the decision. The structure of your business (e.g., Sole Proprietorship, Limited Liability Partnership, Private Limited Company) has long-term implications for **taxation, liability, compliance** obligations, and how you can raise funds.

- **Action Step**: Assess your startup's size, scope, and growth plans. Seek professional advice to choose the best structure that fits your needs, protects your personal assets, and offers tax advantages. Each structure has its own pros and cons regarding liability, taxation, and flexibility.

2. Maintain Proper Documentation and Record-Keeping

- **Precaution**: **Poor record-keeping** can lead to discrepancies, missed tax deductions, or penalties. A lack of proper financial documentation can also trigger audits and complications with government authorities.

- **Action Step**: Use accounting software or hire a professional accountant to maintain detailed and organized records of all transactions, invoices, and receipts. Make sure that you're tracking both **business income** and **expenditures**, and keep **supporting documents** for tax returns.

3. Register for the Correct Taxes

- **Precaution**: Not registering for the necessary **taxes** like **GST**, **Income Tax**, or **Employee Provident Fund (EPF)** can expose your startup to fines and other legal issues.

- **Action Step**: **Register your business with the relevant tax authorities** (such as GST registration, Income Tax, and others based on the nature of your business). Ensure that you know the thresholds and requirements for registration, and do so as soon as you meet the criteria, even if you're still in the early stages of your business.

4. Stay Updated with Tax Regulations and Government Schemes

- **Precaution**: **Tax laws** and **government schemes** often change, and failing to stay informed about these changes can lead to compliance gaps or missed opportunities for tax savings.

- **Action Step: Regularly check updates from tax authorities** like the **Income Tax Department** and **GST Council**. Subscribe to official newsletters or updates related to the government's **Startup India Scheme** and other relevant schemes that may benefit your business. Additionally, consult with a tax professional to stay current on changes in regulations.

5. Timely Tax Filing and Compliance

- **Precaution**: Missing deadlines for **tax filings**, **GST returns**, or **TDS payments** can attract penalties, interest charges, and scrutiny from tax authorities.

- **Action Step: Create a compliance calendar** with all relevant filing deadlines (monthly, quarterly, and annually) for **GST returns, income tax returns, TDS filings**, and other statutory filings. Set reminders to ensure that all filings are done on time. Timely compliance can help you avoid late fees and maintain a good standing with the authorities.

6. Separate Personal and Business Finances

- **Precaution**: Mixing **personal** and **business finances** can lead to tax complications, errors in record-keeping, and challenges in obtaining loans or investments in the future.

- **Action Step**: **Open a separate business bank account** for all business-related transactions. Maintain clear distinctions between **personal and business expenses**. This will help in accurate bookkeeping and make it easier to file taxes.

7. Keep Track of Employee Benefits and Labor Law Compliance

- **Precaution**: **Labor laws** are stringent, and non-compliance can lead to hefty fines or legal issues. You must comply with various **employee welfare** regulations, such as **Provident Fund (PF)**, **Employee State Insurance (ESI)**, and **Gratuity**.

- **Action Step**: If you have employees, ensure that you comply with **labor laws** regarding wages, statutory deductions, working hours, and other employee rights. Register for necessary schemes like **EPF**, **ESI**, and others, and maintain proper records of employee benefits. Failure to do so could lead to labor disputes or fines.

8. Regularly Reconcile Accounts and Financial Statements

- **Precaution**: Failing to regularly **reconcile accounts** can lead to errors in financial reporting, missed deductions, and incorrect tax filings.

- **Action Step**: Make sure to **reconcile your books** on a monthly or quarterly basis to ensure that your financial statements are accurate. This includes reconciling **bank statements** with accounting records, checking **account balances**, and ensuring **accurate profit-and-loss statements**. Regular reconciliation will allow you to catch errors early and avoid future complications.

9. Understand Tax Deductions and Exemptions

- **Precaution**: Not understanding or utilizing available **tax deductions and exemptions** can result in paying more taxes than necessary.

- **Action Step**: Familiarize yourself with the **tax exemptions** and **deductions** available for startups, such as:

  - **80-IAC** deductions for businesses in certain areas.

  - **Startup India Scheme tax exemptions**.

  - **Section 35AD** for capital expenditure in certain sectors. Consult with a tax professional to ensure you're taking advantage of all possible deductions and exemptions based on your business type and location.

10. Ensure Your Contracts Are Legally Sound

- **Precaution**: **Poorly drafted contracts** can lead to legal disputes, unclear terms, and confusion, especially when dealing with clients, suppliers, or investors.

- **Action Step**: Have **proper legal contracts** for business transactions, including **partnership agreements**, **supplier contracts**, and **client agreements**. Make sure that all terms are clearly outlined, and have them reviewed by a lawyer or legal professional. This will reduce the chances of legal disputes down the road.

11. Plan for Tax Audits

- **Precaution**: Many businesses fail to properly prepare for the possibility of a **tax audit**, which can be stressful and time-consuming if your records aren't in order.

- **Action Step**: Stay prepared for a **tax audit** by maintaining thorough documentation and accurate records. Regularly review your accounting practices and ensure your business complies with all **tax filing requirements**. If required, work with a professional who can guide you through the process should an audit occur.

12. Protect Intellectual Property

- **Precaution**: As a startup, intellectual property (IP) can be one of your most valuable assets. Not protecting it early on can expose your business to legal challenges and potential theft.

- **Action Step**: **Register your trademarks, copyrights**, and **patents** to safeguard your business's unique products, logos, and ideas. This ensures that your intellectual property is legally protected and can be defended in case of infringement.

13. Be Transparent with Investors and Stakeholders

- **Precaution**: Lack of transparency with **investors**, **partners**, and **stakeholders** about financial health and compliance could lead to trust issues or loss of investment.

- **Action Step**: Maintain **open lines of communication** with your investors or business partners. Provide them with accurate and timely financial reports, including tax filings, balance sheets, and income statements. Transparency fosters trust and can improve relationships with stakeholders.

Conclusion: Precautions Lead to a Stronger, Sustainable Business

By taking these **precautions**, startup founders can ensure that their business remains compliant with the law, operates efficiently, and takes full advantage of available tax-saving opportunities.

The key takeaway here is that **proactive planning** is essential to ensure long-term success. Compliance isn't just about avoiding fines—it's about building a **strong foundation** for growth, scalability, and sustainability. Taking the right precautions early on helps set up your startup for a future of **growth**, **reliability**, and **financial health**.

CHAPTER 11

CASE STUDIES AND SUCCESS STORIES

This chapter will help entrepreneurs understand how theoretical concepts and strategies are applied in practical, real-world scenarios, offering valuable lessons and insights from successful startups.

Real-world examples are a powerful tool for learning. They not only illustrate the effectiveness of the strategies discussed in previous chapters but also provide inspiration and practical insights for entrepreneurs looking to scale their businesses.

In this chapter, we will examine several case studies and success stories of startups in India (small startups in tier 3 cities also get benefits) that have successfully implemented cost-saving and tax-planning strategies.

11.1 Case Studies of Few Small Enterprises

Each case study will focus on the unique challenges faced by the startups, the strategies they employed to overcome these challenges, and the results they achieved.

These success stories will demonstrate how applying the right tax-saving strategies and cost-management techniques can lead to substantial savings, better profitability, and business growth.

Case Study 1: Zomato - Leveraging Tax Benefits for Growth

Industry: Food Delivery and Restaurant Aggregator

Founded: 2008

Location: India

Key Strategy: Maximizing tax exemptions, strategic investments, and cost optimization

Overview:

Zomato, one of India's leading food delivery platforms, started as a small restaurant discovery service and expanded into food delivery and subscription services.

Challenges:

1. Zomato had to manage rapid expansion across multiple cities and countries.

2. Cash flow management was critical in the early stages, especially with high customer acquisition costs and infrastructure expenses.

3. The company needed to balance growth with the need to optimize tax payments while scaling globally.

Tax and Cost-Saving Strategies:

1. **Startup India Tax Exemptions**: By being recognized as a
    startup under the **Startup India Scheme**, Zomato benefited
    from a **3-year tax holiday**, which allowed the company to
    reinvest more money into scaling its business operations rather
    than paying taxes.

2. **Capital Gains Tax Exemption**: Zomato attracted venture
    capital investment, which qualified for tax exemptions under
    the **capital gains tax exemption** for investments made in
    eligible startups.

3. **Cost Optimization**: Zomato implemented automation tools
    for its operations, reducing manual intervention and
    operational overheads. Additionally, it streamlined its logistics
    by investing in a data-driven approach to route optimization
    and delivery scheduling, thereby saving costs in delivery
    operations.

4. **Use of Technology**: Zomato's app and technology platform
    helped it manage inventory more efficiently and leverage
    customer data to improve the efficiency of its marketing spend.

Results:

- The tax savings allowed Zomato to reinvest in technology and
  marketing, driving both customer acquisition and retention.

- The cost-saving measures in logistics helped Zomato improve its profitability margins despite operating in a highly competitive market.

- As a result, Zomato grew rapidly and went public in 2021, raising significant funds to further expand its market reach.

Lessons Learned:

1. Leveraging government schemes for startups can be critical for reducing the financial burden during the early years.

2. Operational efficiency, particularly in logistics and customer acquisition, can result in significant cost savings.

3. Proper tax planning can make a huge difference in a startup's ability to reinvest and grow.

****

Case Study 2: A Local Artisanal Food Business - "The Gourmet Basket"

Industry: Food and Beverages (Artisanal Snacks and Beverages)

Founded: 2017

Location: Tier-2 City in India

Key Strategy: Tax exemptions, direct-to-consumer model, and lean operations

Overview:

"The Gourmet Basket" is a small artisanal food company that produces and sells premium, handcrafted snacks and beverages, including organic granola bars, specialty teas, and nut mixes. Their primary market is health-conscious urbanites, particularly those living in smaller cities or towns. Despite being a small business, The Gourmet Basket has managed to grow steadily while keeping costs low and effectively planning its taxes.

Challenges:

1. Limited marketing budget and brand awareness in a highly competitive market.

2. Struggled to manage logistics and distribution costs as a small, growing business.

3. High inventory turnover in a seasonal product market leads to cash flow constraints.

Tax and Cost-Saving Strategies:

1. **Utilizing Startup India Benefits**: Being a food startup, The Gourmet Basket was able to register under the **Startup India Scheme**. As a result, it was eligible for **tax exemptions** for the first 3 years of operation, significantly reducing the tax burden during its critical growth period. This exemption allowed them to reinvest more into their business.

2. **Use of GST Benefits for Small Businesses**: The company registered for **GST** as a small taxpayer under the **Composition Scheme**, which simplified their tax filings and reduced compliance costs. They also took advantage of reduced tax rates for small businesses in the food industry.

3. **Lean Operations**: The Gourmet Basket followed a **direct-to-consumer (D2C)** model, which helped eliminate intermediaries and reduce the costs associated with middlemen. They sold primarily through their website, social media channels, and platforms like **Instagram** and **Facebook**, which kept marketing costs low and allowed them to interact directly with customers.

4. **Cost-Saving in Inventory Management**: The company reduced excess inventory by using a **just-in-time (JIT)** inventory system, which helped them reduce storage costs and minimize waste due to expiration dates. This strategy ensured that they had fresh products available without the burden of carrying excess stock, thereby optimizing cash flow.

Results:

- Tax exemptions allowed The Gourmet Basket to reinvest in improving its product line and expanding its reach through targeted online advertising.

- The direct-to-consumer model saved the company significant amounts in distributor fees, enabling them to offer more competitive prices.

- Lean inventory management helped reduce operational costs, increasing profitability despite limited resources.

Lessons Learned:

1. Leveraging government schemes like **Startup India** and the **GST Composition Scheme** can provide vital financial relief during the initial stages of business.

2. A D2C business model can help small companies reach their audience without incurring the high costs of middlemen and distributors.

3. Adopting lean practices such as JIT inventory management can significantly reduce costs and improve cash flow.

****

Case Study 3: A Local Organic Clothing Brand - "GreenWeave"

Industry: Fashion and Apparel (Organic Clothing)

Founded: 2018

Location: Mumbai, India

Key Strategy: Tax credits, cost-efficient manufacturing, and a sustainable brand story

Overview:

GreenWeave is a small fashion startup specializing in sustainable and organic clothing. They produce eco-friendly apparel made from organic cotton and recycled materials, catering to the growing demand for ethical fashion in India. The company was founded by a couple of young entrepreneurs who wanted to create a sustainable fashion brand while also managing costs effectively.

Challenges:

1. High production costs due to the use of organic materials and the need for sustainable manufacturing processes.

2. Competing in a crowded market of established and emerging fashion brands.

3. Funding constraints made it difficult to scale quickly and invest in marketing.

Tax and Cost-Saving Strategies:

1. **Claiming R&D Tax Benefits**: GreenWeave invested in developing innovative and eco-friendly fabric technologies. The company applied for **R&D tax credits** under **Section 35(2AB)** of the Income Tax Act for its efforts in researching sustainable materials and production techniques. This allowed them to save significantly on taxes and fund further product innovation.

2. **GST Tax Credit on Inputs**: Since GreenWeave is a registered GST business, they were able to claim **input tax credits** on raw materials used in production. This helped reduce the effective cost of producing organic clothing, which would otherwise be higher than conventional garments.

3. **Outsourcing Production to a Small Manufacturer**: Instead of setting up their own factory, GreenWeave outsourced production to a small, established organic clothing manufacturer that already adhered to sustainable practices. This eliminated the need for heavy upfront capital investment and allowed GreenWeave to maintain focus on branding and marketing.

4. **Sustainable Brand Story for Low-Cost Marketing**: GreenWeave used its story of sustainability and eco-conscious fashion to build a loyal customer base through **social media marketing** and **word-of-mouth**. They invested in a small but effective content marketing strategy, focusing on **Instagram** and **Pinterest**, platforms where organic and sustainable fashion has a strong presence. This helped them build brand awareness with minimal marketing expenditure.

Results:

- The tax credits and deductions from R&D and GST input taxes allowed GreenWeave to lower production costs and improve profitability, even in the face of higher raw material costs.

- The company was able to scale by outsourcing production to a manufacturer who shared the same sustainability values, allowing them to focus on growing their brand.

- With minimal marketing spend, GreenWeave gained loyal customers and built a strong online presence, which translated into increased sales and better margins.

Lessons Learned:

1. Startups focusing on innovation (like sustainable products) can benefit from R&D tax credits, which can significantly reduce financial strain.

2. Outsourcing production to specialized manufacturers can help small businesses avoid capital-intensive investments while scaling operations.

3. A strong brand story centered on sustainability can be a cost-effective way to build customer loyalty and drive sales.

****

Case Study 4: A Local Tech Solutions Provider - "TechSparks"

Industry: IT Solutions and Consulting

Founded: 2015

Location: Pune, India

Key Strategy: Profit reinvestment, leveraging government schemes, and strategic partnerships

Overview:

TechSparks is a small IT solutions startup providing software development, digital transformation, and IT consulting services to small and medium enterprises (SMEs). TechSparks focuses on creating customized technology solutions for businesses in the healthcare, logistics, and education sectors.

Challenges:

1. Operating in a competitive industry with established players.

2. Limited marketing budget and brand recognition, making it difficult to acquire clients.

3. Managing cash flow due to delayed payments from clients, which is common in the consulting business.

Tax and Cost-Saving Strategies:

1. **Government Schemes for IT Startups**: TechSparks took advantage of the **Startup India Scheme**, which provided access to various benefits such as tax exemptions on profits, funding opportunities, and faster regulatory approvals. This allowed the company to reinvest more of its revenue into marketing and product development.

2. **Tax Deductions on Software and Equipment**: The company purchased essential hardware and software tools for operations, which qualified for **capital investment deductions** under **Section 32** of the Income Tax Act. This reduced the taxable income and helped TechSparks save on taxes.

3. **Strategic Partnerships with Other Tech Companies**: Instead of expanding its internal workforce, TechSparks formed strategic partnerships with other small IT companies to offer complementary services. This allowed the company to handle larger projects without needing to hire additional employees, which helped manage overhead costs.

4. **Reinvesting Profits into Marketing and Client Acquisition**: TechSparks chose to reinvest its profits into digital marketing efforts such as **SEO**, **Google Ads**, and **LinkedIn outreach** to target potential clients in niche industries like healthcare. This ensured that even with a limited marketing budget, the company could maintain a strong online presence.

Results:

- TechSparks saved on taxes and operating costs through tax exemptions and deductions, enabling them to reinvest in client acquisition and technological infrastructure.

- The strategic partnerships allowed them to take on larger projects and enhance their service offerings without increasing overhead.

- As a result of reinvesting in marketing, TechSparks expanded its client base and increased revenue by 35% in the first two years of operation.

Lessons Learned:

1. Tax exemptions and deductions under schemes like **Startup India** can provide much-needed cash flow during the early stages of a startup's lifecycle.

2. Forming partnerships with other businesses can help small companies scale without incurring high operational costs.

3. Reinvesting profits into marketing and business development can help a small company achieve sustainable growth even with limited resources.

****

Case Study 5: A Local Handmade Soap Business - "Pure Glow"

Industry: Personal Care (Handmade Soaps and Organic Skincare Products)

Founded: 2019

Location: Small Town in Uttar Pradesh, India (Tier-3 City)

Key Strategy: Tax exemptions, cost-effective production, local marketing, and leveraging word-of-mouth

Overview:

"Pure Glow" is a very small, homegrown business that produces handmade soaps and organic skincare products. Located in a Tier-3 city, this small business caters primarily to local customers but has started gaining traction through online sales. The business is run by a young couple who decided to create a natural alternative to commercially produced soaps, with an emphasis on quality and eco-friendly ingredients.

Challenges:

1. Operating in a small town with a limited customer base, which restricted immediate sales opportunities.

2. Lack of brand recognition and competition from larger commercial brands in urban markets.

3. Limited budget for marketing, product development, and scaling operations.

Tax and Cost-Saving Strategies:

1. **Registration Under GST (Small Taxpayer Scheme)**: Since "Pure Glow" was starting out, they opted for registration under the **GST Composition Scheme**, which allowed them to pay taxes at a **reduced rate** and simplify the process of tax filing. This move helped them save on compliance costs and avoid the complexities of regular GST filings. It also allowed them to claim **input tax credits** on raw materials like oils, herbs, and

essential oils used in production, thus reducing the overall cost of goods sold.

2. **Utilizing the "Startup India" Exemption**: Although they weren't recognized as a large-scale startup, "Pure Glow" applied for **Startup India registration** since it was still in its nascent stage and had a unique business proposition with organic products. The startup was eligible for tax exemptions on profits for the first three years, which allowed them to retain more earnings and reinvest in the business. This exemption was crucial in the early years when the business was struggling to break even.

3. **Home-Based Manufacturing to Minimize Overheads**: To avoid high rental costs and overheads associated with setting up a factory, the couple decided to manufacture the soaps from home. By using their own space, they minimized fixed costs and worked with low-scale production techniques. They also reduced utility costs by making the soaps in batches rather than setting up a large production line. This helped keep their unit economics tight and their profit margins healthier.

4. **Utilizing Local Resources for Marketing**: Operating in a smaller town, "Pure Glow" could not afford expensive advertising. Instead, they focused on **local marketing** methods, such as word-of-mouth referrals, local community events, and social media platforms (primarily Facebook and Instagram). They joined local women's groups and wellness communities,

offering free samples in exchange for feedback and testimonials. This strategy helped them build local brand loyalty and expand their customer base through personal recommendations.

5. **Cash Flow Management and Lean Operations**: The founders paid close attention to **cash flow management**. They kept tight control of inventory by producing soaps in small batches, ensuring that they did not overstock products, which could lead to spoilage or excess inventory costs. They only made enough stock to fulfill local orders and a few online deliveries each month. Additionally, they set payment terms with customers to ensure that their cash flow was stable and that they did not face delays in payments that could hinder their operations.

Results:

- The GST Composition Scheme and Startup India exemptions allowed them to save a significant portion of their revenue, which they reinvested into improving product quality and launching new products like organic body scrubs and lotions.

- By working from home and producing in small batches, "Pure Glow" managed to keep operational costs minimal. This helped them maintain healthy profit margins despite the small scale of the business.

- Through local marketing strategies and leveraging community support, the brand became well-known in their small town.

Their online sales also increased gradually, reaching a broader customer base from nearby cities.

- The organic and eco-friendly nature of the products resonated with local consumers who appreciated the quality and transparency of the brand. Over time, the business built a loyal customer base, and repeat purchases became a significant portion of its revenue.

Lessons Learned:

1. Even small businesses in Tier-3 cities can benefit from government schemes like **Startup India** and **GST Composition**, which can reduce tax burdens and improve cash flow.

2. Lean operations and producing in small batches helped "Pure Glow" control costs while maintaining quality. This approach allowed them to scale slowly but steadily without incurring significant financial risks.

3. Word-of-mouth marketing and engagement with local communities can be extremely effective for small businesses.

4. Maintaining tight control over cash flow, particularly in the early stages, is crucial for small businesses.

11.2 Conclusion: Key Takeaways from Small Startup Success Stories

These case studies of small companies demonstrate that with smart tax planning, efficient cost management, and strategic use of government schemes, even small businesses can compete, grow, and thrive in competitive markets.

Entrepreneurs should focus on leveraging available tax exemptions, adopting lean operational practices, and reinvesting profits to scale sustainably.

Key Takeaways:

- Take full advantage of tax exemptions, rebates, and Govt schemes designed for startups and small businesses.

- Lean operations, such as outsourcing, inventory management, and strategic partnerships, can help reduce costs and improve profitability.

- Startups should focus on optimizing operational costs, leveraging technology and automation, and using smart marketing tactics to stay lean and profitable.

- Reinvesting profits into marketing, product development, and talent acquisition can fuel growth without relying on external funding.

These smaller, lesser-known success stories offer valuable lessons for entrepreneurs who are looking to scale their businesses while managing costs and optimizing taxes.

CHAPTER 12

HOW A PROFESSIONAL OR EXPERT CAN HELP YOU

A Professional like a Chartered Accountant (CA), Company Secretary (CS), or Tax Expert can be an invaluable resource for a startup in India, providing expertise across several critical areas of business management. As a professional with deep knowledge of accounting, finance, tax, and business regulations, a professional can help a startup navigate complex financial systems and grow sustainably. Below are some key ways a Chartered Accountant can assist a startup:

1. Setting Up Financial Systems

When starting a new business, it's crucial to set up the right financial infrastructure. A CA can help entrepreneurs:

- Establish accounting systems: A professional can assist in setting up an effective accounting system to track expenses, revenue, and profits. This ensures that the startup's finances are in order from day one.

- Choose the right accounting software: A professional can guide the selection and setup of accounting software that suits the business model, making bookkeeping easier and more efficient.

2. Business Registration and Compliance

The professional can assist in legal and regulatory aspects of business formation, ensuring the startup complies with Indian laws. This includes:

- Business Structure: Professional helps determine the most suitable business structure (Sole Proprietorship, Partnership, Limited Liability Partnership (LLP), Private Limited Company, etc.) based on liability, taxation, and growth aspirations.

- Registering the Business: The professional can help register the business with the relevant authorities (e.g., Registrar of Companies, GST registration) and apply for necessary licenses and permits.

- Legal Compliance: Professionals ensure that the business complies with statutory requirements such as company law, tax laws (Income Tax, GST, etc.), and labour laws. This can prevent legal issues later on.

3. Tax Planning and Optimization

Taxation is one of the most complex and critical aspects of running a business in India. A professional can assist in:

- Tax Strategy: A professional can develop a tax-efficient strategy, helping startups minimize tax liabilities through deductions, exemptions, and credits. They can recommend the best approach to structure salaries, investments, and other financial matters to optimize taxes.

- GST Compliance: The Goods and Services Tax (GST) regime is a significant area where a professional's expertise is valuable. They can guide startups on GST registration, return filing, and input tax credit claims, ensuring compliance and avoiding penalties.

- Income Tax Returns: A professional helps prepares and file income tax returns for the business and its owners. They can also provide advice on tax deductions and credits that startups can claim.

- Transfer Pricing: For startups with international operations, a professional can help navigate the complexities of transfer pricing regulations to ensure compliance with international tax laws.

4. Raising Capital and Financing

A professional plays a crucial role in helping startups raise capital and manage their financial resources:

- Financial Planning & Forecasting: A professional can help prepare financial forecasts, cash flow projections, and profitability analyses to present to investors, banks, or venture capitalists. This enhances the startup's credibility and increases the likelihood of securing funding.

- Debt Financing: When a startup is looking to raise capital through loans or lines of credit, a professional can assist in preparing loan applications, reviewing loan terms, and ensuring that the terms are favourable for the business.

- Equity Financing: A professional can help with preparing financial documentation, such as pitch decks or financial statements, that investors may require before offering equity investments.

5. Managing Business Expenses and Cost Control

Startups often operate with limited budgets and need to carefully manage expenses. A professional can help by:

- Budgeting and Cost Management: Professionals can assist in setting up budgets, forecasting costs, and controlling expenses to improve profitability. They can identify areas where costs can be reduced and guide the business toward sustainable growth.

- Cash Flow Management: Managing cash flow is crucial for startups, especially in the early stages. A professional can help with monitoring cash flow and ensuring that the business has enough liquidity to cover operational expenses and avoid cash shortages.

6. Financial Reporting and Performance Analysis

A professional can ensure that a startup maintains accurate financial records and generates reliable financial statements:

- Financial Statements: A professional prepares the balance sheet, profit and loss statement, and cash flow statement, which provide valuable insights into the business's financial health. These documents are essential for internal decision-making, investor communication, and loan applications.

- Performance Analysis: The professional can analyse financial data, highlight trends, and assess business performance, providing actionable insights to improve profitability and operational efficiency.

7. Audit and Assurance

An essential function, particularly as the business grows, is to maintain transparency and accountability:

- Internal Audits: A professional can conduct internal audits to ensure that the business's financial practices are in line with industry standards and regulations. This can also help detect any discrepancies or fraudulent activities early.

- External Audits: If required, a professional can facilitate external audits, ensuring the business is compliant with statutory regulations and that financial statements are accurate.

8. Investor Relations and Reporting

As the startup grows, it may attract investors, including venture capitalists (VCs) or angel investors. A professional can help:

- Investor Reporting: Preparing financial reports, valuations, and other documents required by investors for funding rounds or annual reviews.

- Compliance with Investor Agreements: Ensuring compliance with the terms outlined in investment agreements, including the correct allocation of equity and adherence to reporting requirements.

9. Exit Planning and Succession Planning

A professional can also help startups plan for future transitions, such as mergers, acquisitions, or the eventual sale of the business:

- Exit Strategy: Whether the startup is looking to be acquired, go public, or close down, a professional can assist in creating an exit strategy that maximizes value and ensures tax efficiency.

- Succession Planning: For family-owned businesses or founder-led startups, professionals help with succession planning to ensure a smooth transition of leadership and ownership.

10. Risk Management

Startups face various financial risks, including market fluctuations, regulatory changes, and operational challenges. A professional can help manage these risks by:

- Insurance and Hedging: Advising on appropriate insurance coverage to protect the business from unforeseen events.

- Risk Analysis: Helping to identify potential financial risks and recommending strategies to mitigate them.

Conclusion

For an entrepreneur starting a business in India, having a Chartered Accountant by their side can be a game-changer. From setting up the business structure and ensuring tax compliance to raising capital and managing cash flow, a CA can provide the necessary financial expertise and strategic advice that is critical for the growth and sustainability of the startup. By outsourcing accounting, tax, and financial management to a skilled CA, entrepreneurs can focus on scaling their business with confidence, knowing that their financial matters are in expert hands.

CONCLUSION & FINAL THOUGHTS

Ensuring compliance and maximizing growth potential are pivotal for the success of any startup, and as we have seen, a structured approach to taxation, cost-saving, and legal compliance can lay the foundation for long-term business sustainability. Let's now recap the crucial takeaways and provide actionable advice for entrepreneurs who wish to move forward and implement these strategies in their startups.

Final Tips for Ensuring Your Startup's Compliance and Growth

Starting and running a business involves numerous challenges, especially in the early stages. However, there are some crucial actions that every startup founder can take to ensure their business complies with legal regulations and maximizes its growth potential:

1. **Stay Informed About Regulatory Changes**:

Government regulations and tax laws often evolve. Stay up to date on changes that may affect your business by subscribing to official notifications from tax authorities, attending webinars, or consulting with professionals in the field. This helps you avoid compliance-related mistakes that could lead to penalties or missed opportunities.

2. **Seek Professional Advice**:

Engage with experienced chartered accountants, tax consultants, and legal professionals who specialize in startup laws and tax regulations. Even if you are managing everything in-house, consulting with a professional at key milestones (e.g., registration, fundraising, or scaling) can save you from costly mistakes.

3. **Timely Registration and Filings**:

Ensure that all business registrations (e.g., GST, company registration, etc.) are done in a timely manner. Missing deadlines or failing to file the necessary returns can result in penalties, fines, and, in some cases, suspension of operations. Maintain a strict filing calendar and delegate responsibility to ensure filings are always up to date.

4. **Adopt a Scalable Business Model**:

Set up your operations in a way that allows for flexibility and scalability. This involves choosing the right technology stack, keeping overhead costs low, and implementing efficient processes that can grow with the business. A scalable business model will not only help you reduce costs but also adapt quickly to market changes.

5. **Build a Strong Financial Foundation**:

Financial discipline is key to growth. Keep meticulous financial records, track expenses carefully, and maintain a healthy cash flow. Make sure that all tax-saving opportunities are being leveraged, and reinvest profits back into the business for future growth. For instance, utilizing tax exemptions and credits available under various government schemes can boost your cash flow during the crucial early years.

6. **Utilize Government Support Programs**:

Programs such as **Startup India**, **MSME schemes**, and others provide tax exemptions, funding support, and regulatory relaxations that can significantly help your startup in the initial stages. Leverage these to reduce financial pressure and streamline your operations.

Recap of Key Takeaways for Entrepreneurs

1. **Tax Planning is Essential**:

Efficient tax planning is crucial for startups. Understanding your eligibility for exemptions (e.g., under **Startup India**), leveraging tax credits, and using schemes such as the **GST Composition Scheme** can help you reduce your tax burden and maximize your profitability.

2. **Lean Operations Lead to Long-Term Growth**:

Focusing on lean and efficient operations (such as outsourcing non-core tasks, managing inventory efficiently, and reducing unnecessary expenses) will help startups keep costs low and avoid debt accumulation.

3. **Compliance is Key to Sustainability**:

Compliance with legal and regulatory requirements is fundamental. From registering your company to filing taxes on time, ensuring all paperwork is accurate and timely can prevent avoidable fines and penalties that can harm the business's reputation and growth prospects.

4. **Cost-Saving Strategies**:

There are numerous ways startups can save on costs. For example, choosing a cost-effective office space, reducing fixed overheads, and negotiating better terms with suppliers can help increase your bottom line. Also, tax-saving strategies, like deductions for business expenses and capital investments, can directly improve cash flow.

5. **Building a Strong Brand Presence**:

Successful startups focus on building a brand presence early. Whether through **social media**, **word-of-mouth marketing**, or local community engagement, every startup needs to establish its identity and connect with customers.

6. **Invest in Talent and Technology**:

Talent acquisition and technology adoption can significantly accelerate a startup's growth. Use your available resources wisely — invest in technology that helps streamline operations and hire talented individuals who bring value to the company.

Encouraging Startups to Build a Strong Foundation for Success

Building a successful startup is more than just creating a product or service—it's about laying down a solid foundation that supports the business in the long run. This foundation is built upon several key pillars:

1. **Strong Financial Management**:

This is the backbone of any successful business. Proper financial management ensures that your business can survive difficult times and thrive during growth periods. Keeping track of your cash flow, expenses, and profits and planning for taxes early on will set you up for stability.

2. **Compliance as an Ongoing Process**:

Compliance isn't a one-time event but a continuous process. Ensure that your business complies with the necessary regulations year-round. Keep abreast of changes in tax laws and legal obligations and always have the necessary documentation and filings in place.

3. **Establishing a Robust Network**:

Networking with mentors, other entrepreneurs, and industry professionals is essential. Not only can these connections provide insights, partnerships, and opportunities, but they also serve as a great sounding board when challenges arise.

4. **Customer-Centric Approach**:

Customer feedback and satisfaction should be at the heart of every decision. Create processes for gathering customer feedback regularly and implementing improvements based on that feedback. Satisfied customers are more likely to become repeat clients and spread positive word-of-mouth.

Practical Insights from Real Startup Journeys

Based on real-world experience, here are some frequently encountered challenges and essential tips for startups:

- **Choosing the Right Firm Name & Structure:** Your business name significantly influences how your brand is perceived. It should reflect your business nature and long-term vision. After evaluating growth potential and strategic needs, many opt for a Private Limited Company with two directors to enable future partnerships and credibility.

- **Compliance is Ongoing, Not One-Time:** While registering a Pvt Ltd or LLP adds structure and value, it also brings periodic compliance responsibilities. Be prepared to meet regular ROC, GST, TDS, and Income Tax deadlines.

- **Engage the Right CA Early On:** A knowledgeable Chartered Accountant helps you register correctly with MCA, obtain necessary licenses, and ensure your setup aligns with long-term goals.

- **Survival Needs Patience and Clarity:** The startup journey is competitive and challenging. Stay focused, patient, and consistent with your core objectives—results follow commitment.

- **Customer Retention is Key:** Acquiring customers is important, but retaining them ensures recurring revenue and long-term success. Prioritize excellent service and strong client relationships.

- **Clean Accounting is Critical:** Even a small accounting error can lead to reputational or compliance issues. Maintain accurate records and reconcile regularly.

- **Timely Filings Prevent Penalties:** Missing filings like GST, PT, or TDS can attract hefty penalties. Set up reminders and work with your accountant to stay compliant.

- **Be Transparent with Your CA/Auditor:** Share complete information about your transactions. This transparency helps resolve issues quickly and legally if any arise.

- **Pay Vendors Promptly:** Timely vendor payments not only build trust but also offer better negotiation power. Your current account may not earn interest, but vendor goodwill is priceless.

- **Track Receivables and Collections Efficiently:** Use tools like Tally, Zoho Books, or Vyapar to maintain proper records of invoices, payments, and outstanding balances.

- **Maintain Proper Documentation:** Systematic invoicing and clear purchase orders prevent disputes and strengthen your financial credibility.

Provide Action Steps for Startup Founders to Implement After Reading

As you conclude reading this book, it's time to take action. Here are clear steps you should follow to move forward and start implementing the strategies outlined:

1. **Action Step 1: Register Your Business**

If you haven't done so yet, ensure that your startup is legally registered and meets the necessary compliance requirements. Choose the right structure (LLP, Pvt Ltd, etc.), register for **GST**, and ensure you have all necessary permits.

2. **Action Step 2: Get Tax-Ready**

Schedule a consultation with a tax advisor to understand the tax exemptions, deductions, and credits available to your startup. Begin setting up a system for managing your finances, including maintaining proper books of accounts and ensuring compliance with tax filings.

3.   **Action Step 3: Implement Cost-Saving Practices**

Review your business operations and identify areas where you can reduce costs without compromising quality. Consider outsourcing non-core tasks, renegotiating supplier contracts, and implementing lean inventory management practices.

4.   **Action Step 4: Reinvest in Your Business**

Use any tax savings or profits to reinvest in growing your business. Whether it's through upgrading technology, expanding your marketing efforts, or hiring key talent, make sure that funds are being used strategically to fuel growth.

5.   **Action Step 5: Set a Marketing Plan**

Begin building your brand's presence. Utilize cost-effective methods, such as **social media marketing**, **content creation**, and **local community engagement**. Focus on building customer loyalty and increasing awareness for your brand.

6.   **Action Step 6: Plan for Scaling**

If your startup is doing well, it's time to think about scaling. Review your business model to see if it is scalable. Look for opportunities in new markets, or consider diversifying your product line to capture additional customers.

7. **Action Step 7: Seek Funding if Necessary**

If you need capital for growth, explore funding options such as **angel investors**, **venture capital**, or **government grants for startups**. Make sure your business plan is solid, and be prepared to pitch your startup effectively.

Final Thoughts

Building a successful startup is not easy, but by ensuring compliance with legal and tax regulations, implementing cost-saving strategies, and focusing on sustainable growth, you can overcome obstacles and pave the way for long-term success. Take the time to build a strong foundation now, and your startup will be well-positioned to thrive in the years to come.

Remember, the key to entrepreneurial success is not just in having a great idea—it's in executing that idea efficiently, managing your resources wisely, and staying compliant with the necessary regulations. The road to success may be challenging, but with the right mindset, tools, and strategies, you can transform your startup into a lasting, profitable business.

CALL TO ACTION 

Congratulations on reaching the end of this book! You are now armed with essential knowledge of taxation, cost-saving strategies, legal compliance, and the best practices for building a successful startup. But the real work begins now.

Take action today!

1. **Start by implementing the strategies** you've learned here. Whether it's registering your business, setting up tax-saving measures, or optimizing your operations, begin the process step-by-step. Don't wait for the "perfect" time—take small, consistent actions, and you will see results.

2. **Get professional help** if needed. While this book provides a solid foundation, having an experienced chartered accountant or tax advisor by your side will ensure that you're on the right track and compliant with the latest regulations.

3. **Join the startup community**. Networking with other entrepreneurs, attending events, and continuously learning will help you stay motivated and informed.

4. **Reinvest in your business**. Growth requires resources, so use the profits you generate wisely—invest in your product, marketing, and team to create a strong foundation for scaling.

Remember, **success is a journey**. The road may not always be easy, but with the right strategies, persistence, and mindset, your startup can thrive. **Start today, and build a future that matters.**

If you have any questions or need personalized advice, **don't hesitate to reach out** to me or any professional in the field to guide you further. Together, we can help your startup reach its full potential.

Good luck, and let's make your entrepreneurial journey a success!

A SMALL REQUEST 

Acknowledgment of Errors: The author and publisher shall be obliged if the errors are brought to their notice to carry out corrections in future editions.

Feedback and Suggestions: For any feedback and valuable suggestions, you can mail at:

fca.meghajain@gmail.com OR **ca.meghajain@outlook.com**

Connect with the Author: If you have questions or want future updates in relation to the topics covered in this book further, you can reach the Author at:

Scan QR code

WhatsApp contact